RT ONE
JUICE
OME

BOB MARLEY
REBEL MUSIC

PHOTOGRAPHS BY KATE SIMON

GENESIS PUBLICATIONS
SINCE 1974

REBEL MUSIC

BOB MARLEY & ROOTS REGGAE

PHOTOGRAPHS BY KATE SIMON

This book was first published by Genesis Publications Ltd in 2004 as a limited edition of 2,000 numbered copies signed by Kate Simon. Copies numbered 1 to 350 inclusive were Deluxe copies bound in full leather and additionally signed by Eric Clapton.

The original essay 'Hail' copyright © 2004 Fred Schruers.
'Marley's Farewell' is extracted from a feature that first appeared in the *Washington Post*, 21 May, 1981 written by Fred Schruers.
'Dread No Dead' first appeared in *Interview* magazine, 1978, written by Glenn O'Brien.
Quote on page 28 by Roger Steffens taken from *Photos of the Century*, Capa Agency.
Quote on page 57 by Lester Bangs taken from 'Innocents in Babylon', first published in *Creem*, 1976. Reprinted with the kind permission of his estate.
Selected Bob Marley quotes taken from an original interview conducted by Randall Grass, Warwick Hotel, 1979.
Joe Strummer and Lee Perry quotes courtesy of Bruno Blum.
Aston 'Family Man' Barrett quotes courtesy of Elizabeth Barraclough.
Chris Blackwell quotes courtesy of Fred Schruers.
Recording chronology reprinted with the kind permission of Roger Steffens.

10 9 8 7 6 5 4 3 2 1

ISBN 978-1-905662-82-1

genesis

Genesis Publications Ltd
Genesis House,
2 Jenner Road, Guildford,
Surrey, England GU1 3PL
www.genesis-publications.com

CONTENTS

CONTRIBUTORS

ELIZABETH BARRACLOUGH: A protégé of music business legend Albert Grossman, Elizabeth recorded two albums for his Bearsville Records label. It was Albert who brought Elizabeth and Kate Simon together, aware of their mutual love of reggae, and they later attended the One Love Peace Concert together. Elizabeth was the longtime partner of blues great Paul Butterfield and went on to become a student of history, gaining a Masters degree. She interviewed Aston 'Family Man' Barrett for *Rebel Music*.

ASTON 'FAMILY MAN' BARRETT: Nothing short of a legend in the music business. Family Man – along with his brother Carlton – was part of Lee 'Scratch' Perry's rhythm section, The Upsetters. They were respected as the best rhythm section in Jamaica, Bob Marley was quick to poach them for The Wailers after they fell out with Perry. Family Man became Bob's musical collaborator and band leader, responsible for arrangements and the pulsating bass that was literally the base of The Wailers' sound.

CHRIS BLACKWELL: Often revered as the man who brought The Wailers to the world at large. Sometimes reviled as the man who broke the original trio up. The truth is that without Chris, Bob Marley, Peter Tosh, Bunny Wailer and countless other Jamaican artists would never have enjoyed the international success and recognition that they did. In the early Sixties he was responsible for releasing ska and rocksteady records in the UK – including Millie Small's 'My Boy Lollipop' – before founding Island Records. With artists like Steve Winwood, Traffic and John Martyn, Island became one of the biggest and most respected rock labels in the world. In 1973 Chris signed The Wailers. He became the first member of the music establishment to treat reggae with the same respect as rock music. Chris's marketing know-how, sensitive production suggestions and, most importantly, his appreciation and understanding of the music itself, were integral components of Bob's success around the world.

SPENCER DAVIS: In 1963 Spencer founded The Spencer Davis Group – in the process recruiting a very young Steve Winwood. He achieved international success with such hits as 'Keep On Running' and 'Gimme Some Lovin'' – the former written by Jamaican songwriter Jackie Edwards. By the mid-Seventies he was working for Island Records, which is where he first came into contact with Bob Marley. Spencer passed away in 2020.

JUNIOR DELGADO: Growing up in Kingston, Junior was a regular face on the Seventies Jamaican music scene. His recording career began as part of the vocal trio Time Unlimited. Their first records were produced by Lee 'Scratch' Perry but Junior later found commercial success and critical acclaim with his first solo album, *Taste Of The Young Heart*, in 1979. Through the years, he worked with everyone who was anyone in reggae including Scratch, Niney Holness and Augustus Pablo. He became an elder statesman of roots reggae and remained a successful recording artist and popular live act until his death in 2005.

NEVILLE GARRICK: Neville was responsible for the image of The Wailers and all their artwork from *Rastaman Vibration* onwards – the hessian sack covering of which was groundbreaking in terms of album packaging. Though not a band member in the strictest sense – he occasionally played percussion on stage – he is still considered a bonafide Wailer, responsible for interpreting the music in his artwork and the lighting of live shows. His work with Bob has gained him worldwide respect as an artist. He has remained involved with The Wailers and The Marley Foundation and a collection of his photographs has been published in *A Rasta's Pilgrimage: Ethiopian Faces Places.* He was a founder and executive director of the Bob Marley Museum.

ANTONIO 'GILLIE' GILBERT: Gillie met The Wailers when they were still The Wailing Wailers, drawn to them by their belief in Rastafarianism and love of football, both of which he shared. Gillie became a professional player and he and Bob would often train and play together. Also a talented cook, Gillie would eventually join The Wailers' touring party in 1977 preparing their ital food. He went on to run a recording studio in Miami where Bob's children frequently rehearsed and recorded.

RANDALL GRASS: Randall first met Bob Marley while working as a journalist. His love of reggae and music in general led him to joining Shanachie Entertainment in 1981 where he is now general manager. Not just an expert in roots reggae, but a true enthusiast, in his time he has been instrumental in securing US releases by the likes of Culture and Alpha Blondy.

DICKIE JOBSON: Dickie grew up in Jamaica where he was fast friends with Chris Blackwell. His sister Diane became Bob Marley's lawyer and when The Wailers first signed to Island, Dickie briefly acted as their manager. In 1983 he directed the film *Countryman* featuring the Rastafarian fisherman of the same name. Dickie died in 2008.

WAYNE JOBSON: As a cousin of Dickie, Wayne was introduced to Bob Marley and the reggae scene at an early age. His band Native recorded with Lee Perry and played at the Reggae Sunsplash Festival. He is producer and DJ at Indie 103.1 Radio in Los Angeles and has worked with the likes of Jimmy Cliff, Keith Richards, Willie Nelson and No Doubt. Involved with the production of VH1's *Behind The Music* episode on Peter Tosh, he also wrote the film *Stepping Razor: Red X* about Tosh, which was nominated for a Canadian Academy Award.

STEVE JORDAN: Described as 'the drummer's drummer' Steve is respected as one of the all-time greats. Neil Young, The Rolling Stones, Bob Dylan, B.B. King and James Brown are just a few of the artists he has played with. Much in demand as a producer, he has worked with such varied artists as Keith Richards, Tom Jones, Robert Cray and The Jon Spencer Blues Explosion. He has also worked with Ziggy and Steven Marley. Steve fulfilled his lifelong dream of playing with 'Family Man' Barrett and The Wailers when he worked as Musical Director of *One Love: The Bob Marley All Star Tribute*, featuring Lauryn Hill, Busta Rhymes, Eve, Queen Latifah, Toots Hibbert, Jimmy Cliff and Rita Marley. Carlton Barrett, The Wailers' gifted drummer, is cited as one of his major influences. Steve is currently a drummer for The Rolling Stones.

DAVID KENNEDY: David met Bob Marley as a youth. As a Jamaican living in Miami, he and his friends gravitated towards Bob's mother's house to see and speak with the great man. He credits Bob for steering him on his life's course. He is now a highly respected producer and engineer having worked with Mos Def and Mary J Blige among others.

LENNY KRAVITZ: In a career of more than 40 years, Lenny Kravitz has continued to be one of the most exciting performers in music. His genre-defying approach to music – fused by everything, from John Lennon to Bob Marley – has continued to capture the soul of millions of fans across the world, and as a result, Kravitz has sold over 50 million albums worldwide. From 1999 to 2002, he won the Grammy Award for 'Best Male Rock Vocal Performance' every year, breaking the record for most consecutive wins in one category by a male artist. In 2011, Kravitz was honoured with one of the highest cultural titles in France. He was made an Officer of *Ordre des Arts et des Lettres* by French cultural minister, Frederic Mitterrand, in Paris. In 2018, Kravitz released his eleventh studio album *Raise Vibration*, and soon after confirmed he is working on a follow-up. In 2022, he published *Lenny Kravitz: The Formative Years, 1989-1993*, a signed limited edition book with Genesis Publications.

DON LETTS: As a young DJ at The Roxy in 1976, Don introduced punks to reggae, and later Bob Marley to punk. In the early Eighties he joined the band Big Audio Dynamite but it is as a film maker that he is best known. He wrote and directed *Dancehall Queen* and won a Grammy for his documentary on The Clash, *Westway To The World*.

JUNIOR MARVIN: Born in Jamaica, Junior moved to the UK with his family when he was still a child. He played in numerous bands and as a session guitarist for many more – including, in time, Bunny Wailer, Burning Spear and Delroy Washington – under the various names Junior Kerr, Junior Hanson and, finally, Junior Marvin.

He joined The Wailers in 1977 remaining with them until Bob's death in 1981. In the Eighties he was instrumental in resurrecting the band with himself on lead vocals. He is still playing and performing and has hosted a reggae show on XM Radio in the US.

GLENN O'BRIEN: A renowned writer and journalist, Glenn has written for countless publications and was the music writer for Andy Warhol's *Interview* magazine. In 2002 he launched his own literary and arts magazine, *The Bald Ego*. He kindly allowed us permission to print his interview with Peter Tosh and Bob Marley, which first appeared in *Interview* in 1978. In 2011, Glenn published *How to be a Man*, a sartorial and etiquette guide for men, and in 2019, *Intelligence for Dummies,* a collection of his essays, aphorisms and tweets was released. Glenn died in 2017.

LEE 'SCRATCH' PERRY: Producer extraordinaire, Scratch worked with The Wailers between 1970 and 1971 to create some of their most brilliant music. Something of an eccentric, he nevertheless proved himself consistently ahead of his time and the recording, mixing and sound techniques he developed – most famously at his Black Ark studios – are still an inspiration to producers and artists today, while songs like 'Return Of Django' are reggae classics. He appears in the book courtesy of interviews with the journalist Bruno Blum. Scratch died in 2021.

KEITH RICHARDS: Over a 60-year career, Keith Richards has been the heart, soul, driving force and the foundation of The Rolling Stones as their co-founder and guitarist. The story of how he met his songwriting partner has been told many times in many ways – 1961, a train platform in Dartford where Mick Jagger stood, mail-order R&B albums in hand, the beginning of a friendship and a life-long collaboration. Simply said, as a guitarist Keith is known as one of the best, his influence on rock and pop music undeniable. Alongside his work for The Stones, he is celebrated for his work as a record producer, his collaborations, songwriting and solo work. He has consistently paid tribute to the musicians and artists that he admires, including Bob Marley. In 2010, he penned his critically acclaimed autobiography, *Life*, and continues to tour with The Stones.

FRED SCHRUERS: Fred started his journalistic career working for *Circus*, joined *Rolling Stone* in the late Seventies and became a senior editor at *Premiere*. He was alongside Kate Simon at Bob Marley's funeral and here we have printed an extract of the report he filed by phone the same day. Fred also interviewed Chris Blackwell and provides an essay sharing his memories of Bob, both exclusively for *Rebel Music*.

PAUL SIMONON: Growing up first in London's Brixton and then in Notting Hill, Paul was surrounded by the music – and culture – of ex-pat Jamaicans from birth. Dropping out of art college he joined Mick Jones and Joe Strummer to form seminal punk band The Clash as bassist. His love of reggae – and his insistence that his record collection take precedence on the jukebox at the band's rehearsal studios – infused The Clash's early output on songs like 'White Man In Hammersmith Palais' and inspired the cover of Junior Murvin's 'Police And Thieves'. It would later inform his own songs, most notably 'Guns Of Brixton' (the riff of which he claims to have written after hearing a reggae version of *Swan Lake*). The Clash would go on to play at the Jamaica World Music Festival in Kingston and record with Lee 'Scratch' Perry and Mikey Dread. Paul is now an artist and still lives in West London.

DANNY SIMS: In the Fifties, Danny opened the first soul food restaurant in downtown Manhattan, a bastion of black commerce – and thus a symbol of black pride and resistance – in an otherwise white-dominated land. It attracted high profile black stars like Harry Belafonte and Sidney Poitier. Soon after, he established himself as an international booking agent for Aretha Franklin and Sam Cooke, as well as Malcolm X. With his business partner, the singer Johnny Nash, he moved to Jamaica in the mid-Sixties and established JAD Records. When Johnny saw Bob Marley singing at a Rasta grounation, it wasn't long before Danny signed The Wailers to a publishing deal. Danny was instrumental in trying to break Bob to an audience outside of Jamaica and the two remained close friends right to the end. Danny died in 2012.

PATTI SMITH: Legendary punk poetess Patti Smith had been writing for *Creem* magazine since 1971 and had several books of poetry published when she found international fame with her acclaimed album *Horses* in 1975. The punk movement that took so much inspiration from *Horses* rarely conjured music of such literacy and intelligence. In 2007, Patti was inducted into the Rock and Roll Hall of Fame and in 2022, Patti was awarded the Légion d'honneur by the French Ministry of Culture, France's highest accolade. In 2010, she released her bestselling memoir, *Just Kids*, chronicling her moving relationship with Robert Mapplethorpe, and the beautiful follow up, *M Train*. Patti is still writing and performing with the same unerring eye for 'truth and beauty' today.

BRUCE SPRINGSTEEN: The Boss. Like Marley, one of very few artists to achieve commercial success while remaining true to the art and craft of their songwriting and their souls. Springsteen has consistently prodded at the raw nerves of America in the same way Marley exposed the realities of Jamaica and the struggles of the black man – and myriad other oppressed peoples – all over the world. Bob supported Bruce playing at Max's Kansas City in New York, 1973.

ROGER STEFFENS: Roger is a journalist, broadcaster and actor who is also arguably the world's leading expert on reggae. Over the past 50 years his famous reggae archive has grown to include the world's largest collection of Wailers-related material. He is co-founder of world music magazine *The Beat*; has written regularly for titles such as *Rolling Stone* and *Spin*; and has contributed the sleeve notes for countless albums and interviewed just about anyone of importance in roots reggae including Peter Tosh, Bob Marley and Bunny Wailer. A committed reggae apostle, Roger also lectures all over the world on the subject of Bob Marley, giving audiences the benefit of his immense knowledge and the chance to hear rare recordings and view unseen video footage. His many contributions to this book cannot be overstated. In 2017, Roger released his book, *So Much Things to Say: The Oral History of Bob Marley*.

JOE STRUMMER: Joe is one of very few people deserving of the title 'legend'. As lead singer for The Clash his reggae/dub/ska influenced songs introduced Jamaican music to a whole generation of white youths who would never otherwise have taken an interest. Those influences can still be heard on his critically acclaimed final album *Streetcore* which features a stunning cover of Bob Marley's 'Redemption Song'. Joe was looking forward to contributing to *Rebel Music*. Sadly, in December 2002, he died before he had a chance to do so. His thoughts on reggae and Bob Marley as recorded by journalist Bruno Blum in the late Seventies are included here instead.

DERA TOMPKINS: A native of Boston, Dera first heard about Rastafarianism from civil rights activist Stokely Carmichael. Her interest was piqued by his description of pan-African socialists and she began studying contemporary Jamaican culture, first visiting the island in 1977. Through poet and musician Mutabaruka she immersed herself in Rasta and reggae, becoming friendly with Bob Marley. In 1980 she was lucky enough to be in Zimbabwe with The Wailers as they played at the independence celebrations. Later, as a medical librarian, her skills were used by Bob's personal doctor to research his illness. Dera's active promotion of reggae music in Washington DC has included hosting annual Marley tribute concerts.

STEVEN VAN ZANDT: Guitarist with Bruce Springsteen's E Street Band until 1984 and again from 1999, Steven turned over much of his life to championing human rights causes in the Eighties. Alongside establishing a successful solo career, he spearheaded the anti-apartheid Sun City project and in 1983 founded the Solidarity Foundation, an organisation aimed at supporting the sovereign rights of indigenous people. Still a vital musical force, in 2017 he released his first new album in over 15 years, *Soulfire* and in 2019 he released his first album of original songs, *Summer of Sorcery*. He is a member of the Rock and Roll Hall of Fame and recognised internationally as one of the world's foremost authorities on Rock and Roll.

JEFF WALKER: Jeff was head of publicity for Island Records for four years during the Seventies. He handled publicity for not only Bob Marley, but Peter Tosh and Bunny Wailer too. He was with Bob in Jamaica immediately following the attempt on his life in 1976. Instrumental in convincing Bob to go ahead with the Smile Jamaica concert just two days later he accompanied him in the speeding police convoy that delivered Bob to the concert.

There are musicians, there are good musicians, there are great musicians, and then there is the Honourable Robert Nesta Marley.

Beyond category and boundaries, Bob Marley started a musical, spiritual, social and political revolution.

He was raw.

He was powerful.

He was vulnerable.

He was uniquely his own.

He was a genius without pretence.

He is legend.

He is why the world knows more about reggae, Jamaica, and Rastafarianism.

Marley gave us the power to get up, stand up. The power to fight for justice, and the power to love through his spiritual lyrics and infectious rhythm. He was also wildly charming, handsome, and charismatic. As intimidating as he could appear, his gracious smile was disarming.

This collection of timeless photographs gives us an up close inside look at this uniquely complex man and brilliant iconic artist, who forever changed the world.

One love...

LENNY KRAVITZ

Sometimes within the flux of human history, there occurs such a surge of optimism, a collective sense of mission, that we are swept in its wake. These moments beget movements – spiritual, artistic and revolutionary – and those that participate are the movement. They are the children of light, the renaissance, the journeyers to the East. In my own time, we became the New Wave, merging with a greater wave emanating from the bowels of Kingston, Jamaica – the Rastafarian movement.

The Rastafarian movement offered a spiritual and aesthetic statement, striking a chord with a generation ready for change. It introduced the outsider who exhibited pride in self possibility. Culture was an expression of the people's belief system, art, and even sense of style. Their dreads, sport-sweats and peacetime fatigues. Their colours – the red, yellow and green – of the flag of Ethiopia. The sacred smoke of their God-given herb, the source of divine vision. Their phonetic poetry, distinctive patois and the musicality of the Jamaican language. Their sense of phrasing – I and I – a reference to one's self and to one's place in the spinning order of the universe.

They descend in mind or blood from the Lost Tribes of Israel. The Lions of Zion. They are as the neo-Israelites, searching for the Promised Land. Perhaps the land has always been within them, for the spiritual journey emerging from material poverty is embodied in their music.

When a movement burns bright, what is more emblematic of that brightness than the smiles of their leaders? Kate Simon has captured the likes of Bunny Wailer, Peter Tosh, Lee 'Scratch' Perry, Aston 'Family Man' Barrett, and Bob Marley, who radiated the most recognisable smile of all. He had good reason to smile, for he kept his spiritual sense intact, even at the height of public acclaim, melding the love song with the Rastafarian sense of redemption. One Love. He attempted to bring the warring parties of Jamaica together, and in doing so, set an example for the rest of the world. This period of social, spiritual and political transformation was universally embraced through the power of music.

Kate Simon's photographs possess the atmosphere of those times – the pain and the glory of their revolutionary dream. Kate shot in an honest, direct manner. A fellow worker, she could be found in the trenches with her trusted black body Nikon F-2. She did not seek to expose, but to shoot the picture her subject pictured – the joyful, mutable moments. How fortunate we are to have these images, for they were taken at a time when we were happily swept by a wave, a surge of human optimism, that was infused in the humble heart of a music dubbed 'reggae'.

PATTI SMITH

'Have no fear for atomic energy 'cos none of them can stop the time.'

So often over the years, a lyric of Bob Marley's will come into my mind and help me. He made the truth sound familiar.

But this book is not just about Bob, it's a chance to bring a special era back to life: Jamaica and her musicians from the mid-Seventies until just before the mid-Eighties. Like in a photograph where you have to pull back to get perspective, you need years to realise the value that some things have had on your life. Time ripens the memory. So once more you have a chance to see Carly Barrett playing the drums, to see The Wailers together. To see Jacob Miller swinging in the hammock. To hear Peter Tosh proclaim 'Jah Rastafari!' like only he could.

It's hard to describe what an opportunity it was for a photographer. These personalities were mythic, every last one of them. I've never seen anything like it since. Inevitably, as I was working on this book, it became their tribute.

Certain people, certain times take some of your soul, stay in your soul, are forever part of your soul, and nourish your soul. As a photographer, these subjects encouraged me to grow. They showed me who I could be. They inspired me to do my best. They showed me to myself. The confidence that I gained photographing them was a real part of my growth as a photographer. I was responsible for all the technical stuff myself, whether I was in Jamaica or on the road with The Wailers. This was a real gift.

Now when I think of Bob, I think of many things. I think of how his music doesn't sound dated, how it's still so current. I can still see Bob in my mind, walking down 57th Street right near my studio that day in September, 1980, when he waved at me and exclaimed, 'Kate Si-mon! Wha'appen?' That was the last time I saw him.

When you're working on a book like this, you not only think about it in your waking hours, you think about it while you're sleeping. It becomes part of your psyche. After looking at thousands of negatives of Bob, some of which I had never printed before, I had a dream that Bob was still alive and that he was playing that night. Can you imagine if you could have the chance to see Bob Marley today? What would he be singing about?

KATE SIMON

I was born in Poughkeepsie, New York. As a kid I was into climbing trees and riding bikes; and I was very into watching my father being a photographer. He was a medical doctor, but he loved taking photographs. Oddly enough, the camera that I started my career with he purchased in Jamaica the year of his death.

I went to the Corcoran School of Art in Washington, DC, where I took my first photography class, I was hooked. The moment I graduated I left for England. My mother said, 'You're crazy! What are you going to do for a living?' I said, 'I'm going to be a photographer.'

I had this hunch that that was what I was supposed to be. In fact, I've had these hunches my whole life. I'm sure everyone else must get them too. I've heard Joseph Campbell say that if you look back on your life you'll see that it has a grand design to it.

When I got to London I found a job at the Photographers' Gallery on Great Newport Street. I was an assistant to the director, receptionist, and I handled book sales. I met many well-known photojournalists - David Bailey, Cecil Beaton, Josef Koudelka, Leonard Freed - and I was greatly influenced by them. It was from there that I started my music photography career.

I hadn't really aspired to be a music photographer but I was in London and if you wanted to get paid to take pictures, well... The music industry there, at the time, was so huge. The first photograph I took was printed in *New Musical Express* and was a picture of David Swarbrick, the fiddle player for Fairport Convention. He was in a hospital bed on morphine and my photo credit was Catherine Simon as opposed to Kate.

Dave Fudger, an art director at *Disc*, got me my first proper job. I showed him a picture I shot of Elton John. He liked it and based on that one picture I got a gig as their photographer. After that I shot everybody.

Between 1973 and 1975, you name them, I shot them; from The Rolling Stones, through Led Zeppelin, Stevie Wonder and David Bowie to Black Sabbath and Alice Cooper. I photographed Keith Moon being denied entry to the BBC Club. I would be sent to Rod Stewart's house to photograph him in his latest Bill Gibb sweater acquisition. I would shoot offstage sessions all day and concerts at night. It was a great time.

By 1975 I'd moved up from *Disc* to be the staff photographer at *Sounds*. The best thing about that was I got to go to practically every show in London, including Bob Marley and The Wailers at the Lyceum in 1975. Needless to say, I was floored. KATE SIMON

BLACK CROSS
NURS

What can I say about the Lyceum show? It was shocking. The beauty of his voice; the brilliance of his band; the hypnotic power of the music. For me, it was a calling to reggae. I wasn't prepared for it.

I met Bob for the first time after that show when my friend Anna Capaldi introduced me to him. After that, I'd see him around Fulham where I lived and I'd wave at him and he'd wave at me so I think he got to know my face. **KATE SIMON**

This was one of the first gigs that Don Taylor booked for them, and Taylor had a very shrewd policy: he always under-booked Bob. When Bob could fill a place with 5,000 people he'd put him in a nightclub. If he could play in an arena for 25,000 he'd book him in a place for 10,000. So wherever he played in the first few years of touring with Taylor there were always hundreds or thousands of disappointed fans who couldn't get in, a lot of them milling outside the venue. In the case of the Lyceum there were lines that stretched around the block. You can actually see Don in these pictures, sitting on the stage to Bob's right.
ROGER STEFFENS

The thing about that show is, it was largely attended by black people and they had a hero. And because the white music press were encouraged to go and check him out, they were in on it too, and he knocked everybody's socks off. Whether they were black or white.

There was no pit like nowadays. Five years later he was playing Madison Square Garden where nobody could get that close. At the Lyceum show people were on top of him and that made it great for a photographer because you'd see all the beautiful compositional opportunities of people with their fists raised, crowding round him. **KATE SIMON**

Outside was bedlam. There were people who were waiting in line almost all afternoon and the line was a couple of blocks long. And then there were these dreadlocked guys standing at the entrance saying 'Tickets! Tickets!' and people were just handing them their tickets. These guys would run back into the crowd and sell them. They were hustlers. The result was a near riot and they had to call out the fire department and spray people off the steps of the Lyceum. ROGER STEFFENS

It was one of the first concerts where the people couldn't get in. I remember watching from the dressing room when they had the fire department come and haul people out the door, 'cos there was more people than the place could hold. And it was rocking. In fact, if you listen to that album, the music is a little out; because there was so much energy in the audience they were just hammering on the boards and Carly went with that a little bit, which Bob was kinda upset about. NEVILLE GARRICK

He did a show at the Roxy in LA and when he sang 'No Woman No Cry' I was amazed to see the audience singing along with it. The best live albums are the ones where the audience sings along, so I thought, 'Boy, I'm going to make a live album!' I set it up for when he went to England later in the same year. The show was over two days at the Lyceum, which holds about 2,000 people, I think, and yet you'll find 20,000 people who claim they saw one of them!

But the whole idea really came from hearing people at the Roxy singing along with that song and hearing how the chord sequence sounded like a hymn. It just had a magic. CHRIS BLACKWELL

It became the first live album Bob did and it was a major turning point of his career. That year, 1975, was the year that he became an international star. ROGER STEFFENS

After the Lyceum gig I was so mesmerised that I got into my car and just followed Bob and The Wailers' coach back to their hotel. I'd never done anything like that in my life. I just wanted... I don't know what I wanted. Anyway the coach pulls up outside the hotel and I shuffle in amongst the rest of the Rasta entourage. Entering the large suite I sat quietly in a corner hoping no one would notice. Bob sat at a table in the middle of the room 'reasoning' the night away with older UK Rastas. Eventually the herb ran out. Bob, casting his eyes around the room, sees me in the corner with my little bag and summons me to the table. And so it was, as dawn began to break and my bag began to disappear, that I found myself 'reasoning' with Bob Marley. DON LETTS

To me, it's a very special picture. Bob's face is so open, his smile is so big, his gaze so sharp that the photograph almost seems to give off light. KATE SIMON

GOT TO HAVE *KAYA* NOW

In 1975, Bob Marley wasn't yet the worldwide superstar he was soon to become. If reggae had enjoyed a certain amount of popularity in the UK via its large Jamaican community, most white people's experience of it was still through the film *The Harder They Come* or Eric Clapton's 1974 version of 'I Shot The Sheriff'.

The Lyceum show was a turning point. It made Bob Marley a household name in the UK and his records would soon be climbing the charts in countries all around the world. Yet he was hardly a newcomer to the highs and lows of the music business.

Way back in 1963 when Bob was still a teenager, Bunny Wailer, Peter Tosh and he were known as The Wailing Wailers. Introduced to Clement Dodd - or Sir Coxsone - by Alvin 'Seeco' Patterson, the group went on to record over 80 songs for the legendary ska producer. Their first single, 'Simmer Down', was Number One in Jamaica for two months.

Over the next decade, the three gradually became The Wailers; they wrote songs for Danny Sims and Johnny Nash's publishing company, JAD Records; set up their own label, Tuff Gong; recorded some of their greatest work for Lee 'Scratch' Perry - including the massive Jamaican hit 'Trench Town Rock'; and finally signed with Chris Blackwell's Island Records.

Their first album, *Catch A Fire*, released in 1973, was well received but lit no fires commercially. Their second, *Burnin'*, was released the same year and contained the song that Eric Clapton would make an international hit: 'I Shot The Sheriff'. By the time *Natty Dread* was released in late 1975, both Bunny Wailer and Peter Tosh had quit the group. Credited to Bob Marley and The Wailers, the album was the first to make a serious impression on the UK and US charts and heralded Bob as a major recording artist on an international level. At a time when the rock aristocracy were increasingly seen as tired, worn egomaniacs, this intriguing-looking Rastafarian - an articulate, genuine outsider from a third world ghetto, with firmly held beliefs so at odds with the Western orthodoxy - began to generate serious interest from the media.

Suddenly, Jamaica had been put on the rock 'n' roll map and Kingston's Sheraton Hotel was playing host to interested photographers and journalists from all over the world.

I was down in Kingston in '76 shooting Bunny for his album *Blackheart Man*. One day I was racing Chris Blackwell at the breaststroke in the Sheraton pool. Chris gave me a little bit of a head start but I'd been a junior Olympic swimmer so I was pretty good. But we swam, Chris won, I got out of the pool and there was Bob Marley sitting at one of those tables with tin umbrellas. And that's when I took the *Kaya* portrait.

It wasn't a formal photo session or anything; I was wearing a swimsuit, that's how informal it was. KATE SIMON

For the *Kaya* cover, we were looking for something that was somewhat less threatening and somewhat 'potty' because it was an album where we were trying to widen the audience base. I really liked the photograph, ya know? A smiling Bob as opposed to the more serious, militant ones that we had used before. We were widening the audience and trying to appeal to everyone. With *Exodus* there was no picture of him on the cover at all, so this was kind of a break out thing. NEVILLE GARRICK

The classic shot, the smiley face. That's one of the warmest, most inviting images of Bob ever; so popular as to be chosen as one of the 100 images of the twentieth century. It has become iconographic. ROGER STEFFENS

It was just after Bob's European tour, which established his status as an international superstar. The idea was to cast the net wide; instead of the smoking joint that attracted the hippies and frightened off ordinary people, this was a photo you could show your mother. He looked almost like a boy scout, with his neat hair. This photo now appears on badges, T-shirts, stickers, flags, postcards and plastic buttons. I've seen it at the top of the Grand Canyon, at the entrance to an Indian reservation, in the coffee shops of Amsterdam and on Japanese rugs. The foremost pop critic with the *New York Times* recently said that in 2096, when the former third world has overrun and colonised the former superpowers, Bob Marley will be commemorated as a saint. And Kate Simon's photo will appear on the medallion of Saint Bob Marley! ROGER STEFFENS

I travel around the world a lot and here, there and everywhere you go Bob is a universal symbol. People say you see his image more than you see the Pope's. People embrace him for different reasons but I know in Africa and Brazil, it's like Bob is one of them; it's almost like there wasn't a Jamaica. DERA TOMPKINS

It has been interesting to watch this picture have a life of its own. Everywhere I go all over the world I see this picture that I took. In Antigua, I saw a little boy wearing it on his shirt and the other day I was in a hardware store in Upstate New York and a woman came out of the lighting section wearing it.

I see people embellish it in all kinds of different ways, with all kinds of artistic variations. Maybe they'll put other pictures around it of Marcus Garvey or Haile Selassie or Martin Luther King. I liked the fact that Bob had a stencil of it on his BMW. I saw him wearing the T-shirt of it at the One Love Peace Concert shaking hands with Joseph Hill after the show, so I think Bob liked the picture too.

The biggest compliment I got is from the world in that they wear that picture of Bob all the time. KATE SIMON

Is God who make everybody, and him make a way for the black man that the white man have to follow, because out of the black man came the white man, all white men. BOB MARLEY, 1978

THE WAILING WAILERS

When Bunny Wailer and Peter Tosh left The Wailers in 1973, it cannot have been an easy decision for either of them.

Not only were they finally recording for a major international label, albeit for scant reward as yet, but the three had been singing, writing, working and even living together on and off for the best part of a decade. In that time, they had tasted both success and failure and experienced for themselves the piratical nature of the Jamaican recording industry. Through it all they steered a course with unstinting hard work. The three were like brothers. But the two had their reasons, however mysterious. Bunny was sick of working for nothing and sick of Babylon full stop. Peter? Perhaps Peter was just sick of sitting in Bob's growing shadow. He was a talented and brilliant songwriter in his own right and an accomplished musician and singer; as was proved by his all-too-brief solo career.

Bunny too, though less prolific than either Peter or Bob, made some beautiful music. His album *Blackheart Man* is considered a classic. But despite their respective solo successes, many still regard their finest work (including Bob's) as being done as a trio.

All the music, the collection of The Wailers' music, was perfect. When the original group split it was real bad at the time, because folks were looking up to them just like The Beatles, The Rolling Stones or whatever. They were the group that was gonna put Jamaica on the world stage. Then some spirit came, or some negative vibe came and separated that. But Bob was on a mission. Nothing was gonna stop him, he was on a mission. At the time Bunny said that he wasn't gonna tour, he was just gonna chill; jus' live and vibe as a Rasta. But he did what he had to do. Peter did what he had to do. He went on a soul adventure. His stuff was good too; my favourite was, I think, the *Equal Rights* album. But Bob was just special. ANTONIO 'GILLIE' GILBERT

I was working with Bob [in 1970] and Bob didn't want to go back with the Bunny and Peter t'ing. And I seh well I think you should do it with this soul revolution for special reason. Because the three of your voice blend very good like an angel, to manifest your work on this soul revolution, a spiritual revolution, fighting against government pressure and t'ing like that. So he say I'll take your advice and call 'em back. Otherwise there would be no more Peter and Wailer and the Coxsone t'ing break up. It was my idea to put them back together. He alone didn't want to do it. Bob, he wanted to sing with me alone without them, but I said no, you need them for special work like 'Sun Is Shining'... you need the harmony.
LEE 'SCRATCH' PERRY

I loved the sound of the original Wailers, with Tosh and Bunny. But it was inevitable, with a partnership like that, that something had to be sacrificed. Bob stood out very early on and he emerged as a star early on too. SPENCER DAVIS

It seemed great at first because all three of them could sing and write and make good music together, but in fact it was too many cooks. If the band get on really well it can work, but...

I think Bob saw the bigger picture better than Peter and Bunny, and most of the other artists in Jamaica. I think it was because he'd been abroad and lived abroad and seen a thing or two. By being in Europe at a time when all that rock was happening, he got more of that music than the American, doo-wop, harmony thing The Wailers were doing.

One of the first things Chris did when he signed Bob was to get me to take him on a tour with Traffic in America so he could see what other artists on the label were doing. The general idea with artists in Jamaica at the time, helped along by *The Harder They Come*, was that every producer was ripping you off. I think Chris wanted to show him that people on the label who were making the money were getting the money. So I think Bob had a much wider view; he knew how valuable press was for instance.
DICKIE JOBSON

I took Bob on the road with Traffic, John Martyn and Free who I had touring in America. I took him because I wanted him to see the shows, the number of people that were being drawn by these artists and none of them were based on a single hit. His background was the single hit business; the people he knew in the music business internationally were Danny Sims and Johnny Nash. 'I Can See Clearly Now' was a single hit, but Johnny Nash was never an album artist.

In reggae, nothing was conceived as an album package whereas in the rock world everything was album-based. That world didn't even release singles. Led Zeppelin never really released singles; Pink Floyd did a couple, but Traffic didn't in America. So I decided to adopt the same approach with Bob.

I think what happened with the three of them is that they were three big stars. There were a lot of little jealousies and things, and basically Peter was very erratic. Bob was much more balanced and career-orientated in a way, whereas Peter was a natural wild man. And I respect him for that; he was the real thing, a real wild man! And Bunny was very cautious and very nervous of failure so he just didn't want to leave Jamaica. He didn't like touring, he didn't like being out there and I don't think he particularly liked playing second fiddle a little bit as Bob got bigger and bigger. CHRIS BLACKWELL

Peter is unjustly ignored these days. He had just two songs on *Catch A Fire* and one-and-a-half on *Burnin'*. That's one of the reasons he quit the group. I mean, three songs on two albums for a guy that had a whole heap of great music backed up... I guess that's why the group really broke up because they just couldn't hold all that talent any more. The centre couldn't hold them. Apparently in the last couple of years when Bob was sick, Peter never even picked up the phone to ask him how he was. He didn't talk to him once in the last two years. They fell out. I believe he was intensely jealous of Bob. He felt that he had contributed just as much to the music. ROGER STEFFENS

Oh, I think they each admired and respected one another although of course there were sometimes jealousies... I mean, this is normal. But I think they had each other in their hearts always. I think they were brothers. DERA TOMPKINS

I could never really separate them but it did seem that there was not only enough talent but enough not being said between the three of them that they deserved to be recording separately. In the time I was with them, I certainly did not see any signs of animosity or jealousy, either when they were together or when they were performing. JEFF WALKER

LEGALIZE IT
LEGALIZE 'IT

Once I said: 'Peter, I want you to take me to a place where I can take some pictures of the local culture.' So he took me down to Orange Street, I think it was, and got out of the cab. As a photographer you've got to be intuitive and careful to let a person know, wordlessly, that you're about to take their picture. It becomes second nature to you and you get a feel for whether or not it's OK. So, I walked up to what I thought was a pretty benign setup: a woman selling vegetables. I thought she gave me the green light, but I was wrong because I took one picture and the whole street turned round and chased me. KATE SIMON

Most people who don't know about Peter Tosh feel that he was a dangerous person; unpredictable, mean, frightening and intimidating. And yet my memories of him are of one of the funniest people I ever met who was warm and loving. Except when he started talking about the music business and Babylon. I think one of the reasons he wore the dark glasses so often is so you didn't see the twinkle in the eyes behind all of this. ROGER STEFFENS

I didn't find him at all intimidating as a person. He was charismatic and a great photo subject. I've always liked pictures of Peter doing his karate. He studied it and he was pretty good.

He also had an incredible speaking voice and was the tallest man on the island. When I shot him the first time, lightning went off and he said, 'You see that? I made that happen. Jah, Rastafari!'

These were all taken in Tommy Cowan's yard. Everybody went down there to hang out, play cricket and smoke herb. KATE SIMON

For me, Tosh was the ultimate rock 'n' roll legend. Bob Marley was like Martin Luther King, Peter Tosh was Malcolm X. He was very revolutionary and very funny at the same time. The thing that Tosh had that I felt Marley didn't have was that sense of humour. Everybody thought Tosh was dangerous: no, no, no, no! Bob was more dangerous than Tosh. Tosh was a total comedian. Everything he said was funny, his language and everything about him.

Bob had a very spiritual vibe; very dedicated and disciplined. I just wish he had been a little bit looser, but maybe I wasn't around at the times when he was loose and funny. He was a genius on a mission and I think he was just focused on it, at times forgetting the lighter side of life. Whereas Peter Tosh was always looking for fun, madness and craziness. WAYNE JOBSON

Peter Tosh was not, in the beginning at least, very militant. Bunny Wailer was tougher than Peter Tosh. I would say the first time I saw Peter Tosh show the militancy was when he went with The Rolling Stones' record company. I know he stayed at their house and I started hearing really bizarre stories about things that he did there. But when I'd see Peter in New York – because I did the *Mama Africa* album for him and the last two albums for him before he died – I just never saw that side of Peter. I did see some pretty tough sides of Bunny Wailer.

But mainly I saw them as serious artists. Probably the greatest group of the century. I thought Peter Tosh and Bunny Wailer were geniuses. When I saw those three guys – and Rita Marley – I just didn't believe that they were from this little island. It wasn't like Bob was so far over Bunny, and Bob was so far over Peter; I saw them as equals. It's my feeling that if Bunny Wailer wanted to, he – like Bob and like Peter – would have been just as big on his own as he was in The Wailers because he's got that kind of talent. DANNY SIMS

When Peter signed for Columbia, Chris [Blackwell] very kindly allowed me to continue as Peter's publicist. So for *Legalize It* and, I guess, his first two albums for Columbia, I handled Peter even though he was on a completely different label. As a matter of fact my relationship with Peter was among the most casual of the three. He was extremely friendly and accessible and sweet. He goes in another direction as well, but I always found him to be wonderful to be around. JEFF WALKER

19291

I think Peter was a bit more hardcore, more hard-line and very outspoken, while Bob was more diplomatic and accessible to everyone. He was less arrogant... Actually, I really shouldn't use that word: he was simply more accessible and always a gentleman with people. JUNIOR MARVIN

They were all militant. They all shared the element that brought them together: their faith in Rasta. That's what gave them their world view, their vision, their thoughts, their inspiration. They say, 'Many rivers, one sea.' They were all on the same mission but they just had a different style. I think they shared the same philosophy in terms of their commitment to the black struggle first. We are all about a better world but we have to lift up our family first because we have been suffering for so long, here in Babylon. So they all had a mission to lift up the hearts of scattered African children everywhere. DERA TOMPKINS

Peter's wordplay was fantastic. His manager was his damager, and his producer was his reducer. He called Sly and Robbie, Slime Come Rob Me, or Rye and Slobbie. Blackwell was Whiteworst because, 'If 'im black, show me how 'im black, and if 'im well, show me one thing that is well with 'im. No man, 'im Whiteworst.' Germsmany, Rome in Shitaly, Hellay, Follywood, San Fran-Disco, Folly Fornia, United States of A-sad-ica – because there's nothing 'merry' about A-merry-ca. What kind of a head comes up with these things? Priceless stuff. Fri-ends. You have to pull it apart: first syllable is 'fri' – which means eliminate, burn – and 'end', which is to get rid of you. So be careful of your friends, for they will fry you in the end. And it was an alleged friend who came and killed him. ROGER STEFFENS

I don't see why you should blame Blackwell like Peter did. All this big talking about 'Whiteworst' an' this an' that. Him have a problem. Him have a problem with how him see Bob Marley take off. And him coulda take off too, because it was a group. And he did take off! Because a'what Blackwell had done, he still benefit from the works. And yet all that big, big talk... JUNIOR DELGADO

He's a tricky man that Pete Tosh. I remember we did this Bob Marley festival – I think it was in Montego Bay [World Music Festival, Bob Marley Centre, Montego Bay, 1982]. Black Uhuru were on the bill, Peter Tosh, various other groups and us. We got on and did mostly our reggae-orientated stuff, and then when we came off it was time for Peter Tosh. By this time, it was like five o'clock in the morning and for some reason something went wrong with the equipment. I remember hearing him shouting: 'How come it all work for that heathen group The Clash and not I?' He was a bit pissed off.

He's sort of the extremist of The Wailers in my mind's eye. From what I've read about him; I never met him. But it's one of those elements of the group. All the Wailers had their moments. PAUL SIMONON

Pete Tosh was 42 when he was killed, from 23 rounds of ammunition, on 11 September, 1987. KATE SIMON

The first time I shot Bunny we had to wait a week for him to come down off the mountains – because there were no phones of course – and waiting for Bunny became like *Waiting For Godot*.

There were three of us, a cabal of journalists: Neil Spencer, Vivien Goldman and myself. And we were all going really nuts waiting for Bunny. It was quintessentially Jamaican. 'Soon come.' We waited so long we began to go a little crazy. But when he finally came, I was ready and so was he. I got great pictures. He could kill you with one glance.

I wanted to get more pictures and he agreed. He said I could interview him at the studio, but only if I wore a skirt. I didn't really believe him, but when I turned up he said, 'Kate Si-mon, where's your skirt?' So I left. KATE SIMON

The fact he let Kate shoot those expressions, to me that's very impressive. Bunny doesn't like photographers shooting. He's very, very uncooperative. ROGER STEFFENS

When you got to Jamaica you knew you were in a heavy place. The moment you landed, you could feel it, like there was something in the air. It was Bunny Wailer's record *Blackheart Man* that helped me understand Kingston, helped me understand the environment. I wrote in my journal at the time that it was my guide. KATE SIMON

Bunny's first album, *Blackheart Man*, that's a classic. Another one I liked was the *Rock And Groove* album: that's a good album. He had another one, *Protest*. They were some good albums, but *Blackheart Man* is the one that stood out for me. The *Rock And Groove* album was more kinda dancehall. ANTONIO 'GILLIE' GILBERT

Oddly enough I've been playing *Blackheart Man* a lot recently. It was usually the last record I put on at night. My son – who was only three at the time – came down to Jamaica with us and I used to play it for him when he went to bed. But he was scared by the song 'Amagideon' and Bunny himself reassured him that it was not a song to be scared of and that Armageddon itself was not something to be frightened of. He couldn't have been sweeter. I think it's a milestone record and certainly underappreciated in general. JEFF WALKER

SCHOOL
PHONE

In 1970 The Wailers made what I consider to be the first real reggae album in history, as opposed to a collection of singles. Leslie Kong – who had recorded Bob as a soloist in '63 – had become a millionaire through Millie Small's 'My Boy Lollipop', and 'The Israelites' by Desmond Dekker, each of which sold over four million copies worldwide. The Wailers figured, OK, this guy knows how to play the pop music game. He crossed over, we want to cross over. The Wailers wanted to be Number One on the R&B charts in America more than any other thing in the world, and they thought Leslie Kong could help them do it. So they made an album that was thematically a pep talk to themselves, with songs like 'Go Tell It On The Mountain', 'Do It Twice' and 'Soul Shakedown Party', which was a James Brown riff, with that great line: 'Janie's in the backyard, doin' the outside dance.'

When it came time to name the album, Kong told them that he was going to call it *The Best Of The Wailers* and they flipped out. Especially Bunny. He said: 'Look, we're young men, we have long careers in front of us, so you don't know what the best of The Wailers is. If this is the best of The Wailers to you it must mean you're about to die. So don't do it.' Kong laughed. He put the album out and called it *The Best Of The Wailers* and a week later dropped dead at the age of 37. From that day forward the words of Bunny Wailer had a little extra weight to them, you know? **ROGER STEFFENS**

MARVIN GAYE
"LIVE"
SPIDER-MAN

JAMAICA

When I see a place, I see the people. Seeing the schoolchildren with bows in their hair walking up the road to Strawberry Hill, or the vendors on Orange Street; the rural characters like Jack Ruby in Ocho Rios or the Kingston entrepeneurs like Bunny Lee.

The record shops were like meeting halls where everybody would get together – men, women and children. It was a country rich in subject matter. I don't think I met anyone there who wasn't a complete natural in front of the camera. KATE SIMON

RECORD
RECORD CITY
FOR BEST IN
LOCAL
& FOREIGN
HOT
SHOT
STICK NO POSTERS
RECORD
WELCOME TO
BUNNY LEE
RECORD · CITY
101 ORANGE STREET KGN.
PHONE
92,24648
TRACK PRICE
GORGAN
SOUND
DREAD

Jamaica is the last 45rpm singles market in the world. And every week any number of records come out so it can change like that. There's stuff played at the dances that hasn't even been released. That's very common. There's popular songs that have never been released. There's the whole thing of 'specials', where sound systems will pay an artist to cut a special just for them with singers singing the name of a sound system like Volcano: 'Volcano is the best so/Make sure you don't test volcano/'Cos we'll put you to rest.' RANDALL GRASS

Bucky Marshall, a leading PNP gunman, on the hood of his car in Reema during a short-lived truce. These were people you didn't mess with. KATE SIMON

In certain areas of town these gangs were the government. They ruled the street with guns, cash and with a style and fashion that commanded the respect of the people. Just as Clint Eastwood's characters in the Spaghetti Westerns thrilled Kingston audiences, so did these guys. RANDALL GRASS

Growing up in Brixton, I remember after the Saturday night blues dances, early in the morning, there'd be guys hanging in the street, recovering, wearing these amazing two-tone trousers. I remember going home to my mum saying that I wanted a pair of these sort of orange-brown, sparkly trousers – which is the only way to describe them. I eventually got a pair, but on the first day of playing on the bomb sites with them on, I got a great big hole in the knee.

Reggae wasn't just about roots, it was about aesthetics too. The two-tone suits and Ben Shermans eventually evolved into pin-striped trousers. I think it's because in the Spaghetti Westerns the bad Mexican guys have all got pin-striped trousers. There's a cross-over element that happens. It's a lot to do with, if this is my last night on earth, then at least I'm gonna look sharp! You make sure you're not wearing flared trousers or whatever...

...The first time I visited Jamaica we came over with Mikey Dread. Me and him got on really well because he'd come to my basement flat in London and he was amazed at the variety of reggae records that I had. I read, not too long ago, that he said they were all good records, there were no duff ones, so there was a kind of cultural understanding between us.

Walking round Kingston Town is a bit like walking round Dodge City: it's a tricky place and it's definitely got a slight edge to it if you're a white person – Mikey was my human passport. He'd walk me through the streets and he'd say, 'See that bloke coming towards us, he's been shot 18 times and he's famous all over the island. He caught these people trying to rob a bank and he made them all crawl to the police station on their bellies through the centre of town.' And as we got closer he said, 'Look at his ankles.' And by this point we were introduced and I could see that he had pistols taped to his ankles. He was a real western style hero. It was just fantastic. But you wouldn't get that if you went on a package tour to Ocho Rios or Montego Bay or something. PAUL SIMONON

BOB MARLEY AND THE WAILERS
LEE PERRY
BOB MARLEY
BOB MARLEY

49 LEE 'SCRATCH' PERRY

In a way it can be argued that Scratch was the maestro of the Golden Age of Reggae. He produced The Wailers before they signed with Island and I remember his studio was covered in photographs of all the people he had worked with. When I took this picture he was recording The Heptones, and to see him in the studio conducting his board was really something to see, and feel. Unforgettable. It was like a party but there was some serious music being made at the same time.

After he saw this picture he made button badges out of it and had a big mural of the photograph painted outside Black Ark Studio, where I'd taken the shot. KATE SIMON

Scratch is a genius, but I don't think there's any question in my mind that he is a little insane. But in spite of all of that he's a compelling figure. I don't go to see him live because I don't enjoy it anymore. I've seen him come with tapes and rant for an hour, set his clothes on fire or burn the stage; it's not fun. ROGER STEFFENS

He's a little eccentric! That's how we style it! DAVID KENNEDY

The Black Ark was a school, ya know? That's where all different yout's would come, fe Scratch to record them. But you have to be excellent for Scratch to record you. You have to be really great or you c'yan get a cut. JUNIOR DELGADO

Lee Perry is especially interesting. When I was about nine my parents finally split up and my father left home. Suddenly my stepfather moved in and a couple of months later my mum said, 'We're all going to move to Italy.' So me and my brother went to live in Italy for a year. We didn't go to school, we just played on the streets like we did in Brixton. That's when I was first exposed to Spaghetti Western films. When I finally got back to London and I heard all these Lee Perry songs like 'Clint Eastwood', I felt, 'I know about this, I've seen those films.' He's a character. I've said it before and I'll say it again, he was the Ennio Morricone of Jamaican music.

A lot of his early albums had songs like 'Justice To The People' with babies crying, which is a bit off the wall. You hear it and go, 'Bloody hell! I want more of that!' Then there's songs like, 'Kimble'. That's just amazing! It goes something like: I am Kimble the nimble, you tread on my toes. Ouch! It's really fantastic. That particular sound he had: 'sticky' is the best way I can describe it. Everything just stuck together. It was quite hypnotic and obviously influenced the Rasta culture that came later.

Older guys like The Heptones obviously got all their influences from artists like The Impressions in America. There was a sort of cross over, when black awareness was big. Then everyone started looking at their own culture and that's when the Rasta thing came to the forefront. Suddenly it was, 'We don't have to mimic this or that, we've got our own thing and it's home grown.' Literally. Culturally as well as all the stuff they smoked. PAUL SIMONON

With The Clash we had the echo on the guitars and the dubbing, but if we were consciously trying to get the Lee Perry sound we'd have got Lee Perry in to do it. Of course, we did have him at one point, but it was very difficult for him to sink his teeth into something that was so culturally different. It didn't quite work.

Apparently, after we did the 'Complete Control' session with him, he had a photograph of us on his mixing desk along with Bob Marley and all the other people he worked with, so that was quite an honour.

In later years he came on tour with us. When we played New York, he did a couple of shows and he said, 'Well, Paul, Joe, Mick, when are we gonna go on this world tour?' We were like, what world tour? We've only just got here, you know? PAUL SIMONON

Bob went away, maybe to America, and he never hear that funny sound that I have. He go to England and he hears and come back to Jamaica and said, 'Scratch, we have a song there and honestly I really want to work with you.' I said, 'I don't really want to work with no singer at the moment,' because I was just making instrumentals, and I was really burned and beat off by the Coxsone treatment and I decide to upset. But I look 'pon Bob and it was like somebody send him. Come inside. I didn't want to do it. Definitely. 'Ca I didn't need no help, I didn't need no help from Bob and nobody. A upsetting vibration was good enough for me. But Bob hear it and want to join and I said, 'OK then.' I look and I see that there was someone really send him because him need help.

I said 'Let me hear the songs that you have to sing.' And then he started singing: 'My cup is overflowing and I don't know what to do.' So I said this to myself, 'As a producer listen to an artist's inspiration, this is a true confession, is a truth.' His cup overflowing he don't know what to do so he need help. I didn't say that to him, but I think about it. I didn't want to take him on, 'ca I didn't want to use any singer. 'Cos they was behavin' so to stink, and so rude that I didn't want to get involved, just want to do instrumental.
LEE 'SCRATCH' PERRY

Here you have a person always thinking outside the box. Always blowing out new stuff, always wanting to do new things.
The brother is crazy, but we love him. He's just totally there for the music. STEVE JORDAN

Blackwell gave Wayne [Jobson] $500 as royalties and asked him to give it to Scratch when he got back to Jamaica. And Scratch took it and he says, 'Royalties? This isn't royalties, this is peas. Boil the water, we're gonna have peas tonight!' And he starts eating it. He ate all $500. Swallowed it.

But he was a major force for The Wailers. I was talking with Bunny about the Scratch sessions once – because they still had their own label, Tuff Gong, at that time – and I said, 'How did you decide what to keep for yourself and what to give to Perry?' Bunny said, 'We just gave him the throwaway stuff.' 'Trench Town Rock', 'Kaya', 'Duppy Conqueror', 'Mr Brown', 'Keep On Moving'; all these things they would make over at Island. Unbelievable... the throwaway stuff! ROGER STEFFENS

John [Lydon] and I had the pleasure of watching Lee 'Scratch' Perry conjure up reggae versions of 'Anarchy In The UK' and 'Holidays In The Sun' in a herb haze. I remember them as being sort of cheesy. More bread than dread at the control. But Lee Perry is the Salvador Dali of sound. DON LETTS

After Bob left him, he start acting crazy, I'm telling you. Me and Bob used to go to the studio every Sunday evening, 'cos Family Man was never paid for those albums you know?

And 'Punky Reggae Party' was done there without Bob. Lee Perry brought it to London in '77. After that, he just start messing up the studio. ANTONIO 'GILLIE' GILBERT

Scratch recorded my first demo for me at the Black Ark. One week Robert Palmer was in town and I went down with him to the studio and at the end of the session I just said, 'Hey, I have some songs,' and Scratch say, 'Let me hear them.' I played the songs and he say, 'Come, let's record right now.' He was so mad though. He kept saying to me, 'I wanna work with you 'cos you are an Arawak Indian.' So I said, 'Yessir, I'm an Arawak Indian, let's record!' Whatever he'd have said, I'd have said, 'Yes.' I wanted to work with him so much.

Scratch could say, 'Bananas are God,' and he's worshipping bananas. So, every time I go an' see him I would have to carry a big bunch of green bananas. One day he said, 'Red! Red is holy!' and he paints the whole place red. Then the next week he said, 'Red is evil! Gold is good!' So he repaints everything gold. And then the next week it's green... I think he painted all his master tapes – including all the Bob Marley master tapes – and ruined everything. WAYNE JOBSON

I met him once, 20 years ago, and tried to interview him, as much as you could interview him. He was going through a period of writing everywhere; on walls, on his shirt... He had covered the walls of his apartment with writing and eventually the landlord threw him out because he'd started on the halls!

I think a lot of the madman act was cultivated. People forget, Jamaica was a tough place. I think Scratch did a lot of what he did to keep the vultures there off his back. RANDALL GRASS

He mess up all the tape and burn them. The Congos caused that, and some other people who kept come check-checking, ya know? Congos and him and them kick off and the Congos tell, 'Me want tape, and me want this and me want that.' He get mad and just burn them and splash paint all over the place. JUNIOR DELGADO

NOTICE
THIS IS A PRIVATE HOME
KIDS : WOMEN LIVE HERE SO WE
WONT ACCEPT INDECENT LANGUAGE
IN THIS YARD NO ONE SHOULD ENTER
THE STUDIO WITHOUT CONTACTING
SOME ONE AT THIS FRONT DOOR

He [Bob] didn't have a house 'til I have to give him my house to live. He was living where the Black Ark studio is. I give Bob a room deh in my yard to live, Bob was living there. So Bob was having my front room, and the room that Bob was staying in, that's where I have my genie. I have a real genie. My genie's not in a bottle. The breeze. The bag of breeze. You ever hear about the bag of wind? Maybe you rub a ring and a genie flies out?

So he was living in the genie room and absorbing the power of the genie to do the job because I didn't hear a singer. And he didn't have the personality and the looks and the complexion and the hair. Even though it wasn't Dread when he come. So after him gather the power and him get mighty strong I know it was real power. And he put on the Dread and decided take over. And he did it, he did really take over. LEE 'SCRATCH' PERRY

That's the Upsetter… this is typical a'him; stamping foot hard. JUNIOR DELGADO

My idea one time was to wake up and say I want to imitate God. 'Cos I see myself a two-part; one part of me is good and one part of me is evil. An evil part which could be Satan which is every man. So I chose the right part and say I want to imitate Emperor Haile Selassie. There really one man and say I act and look like him. You think is because I imitate His Majesty I look like him? Could be. LEE 'SCRATCH' PERRY

But this guy was no Rasta, no matter what he or anybody else says. This was an uptown cat. A hipster. With his hair slicked straight back, his greying beard, strutting around cocky and amused, a diminutive lion in his kingdom, he at length danced over to the corner where I was trying to be inconspicuous, squeezed past me, grabbed a bottle, and straightening up, stopped a second to look me in the eyes close as the air, smiling knowingly, and I smiled back. A few minutes later he walked up to me and said, 'You wine man.' It was not a question. 'Sure,' I said. He laughed. 'I know wine man,' and he handed me a plastic cup and a bottle of something called Winecarnes, which is local wine fortified with meat extracts that he seemingly drinks all day without ever losing his stride. LESTER BANGS – FROM 'INNOCENTS IN BABYLON', *CREEM*, 1976

I don't know who this is but he's wearing my Clash photograph. He's outside of Scratch's. KATE SIMON

I was the reggae lunatic in The Clash. That's how I learnt to play bass, by listening to reggae records. Because I'd grown up exposed to that music, the style and the food, it seemed natural for me to play along with reggae. You could hear what the bass was doing, as opposed to music by The Who, The Kinks or whatever. You felt it, you didn't have to figure it out from amongst the loud guitars and thumping drums. PAUL SIMONON

'Punky Reggae Party' is my words, my idea, me write the whole of them. When him [Bob] was in trouble him stuck in Miami, him didn't want to cut off his leg from long time, and he get stuck in Miami [recovering from an operation that removed part of the cancerous big toe on his right foot] and him sent fe call me go Miami, and give him that 'Punky Reggae Party' to sing and him want a wicked big connection between the reggae and the punk. And that was number one giant connection.
LEE 'SCRATCH' PERRY

We went there [Jamaica] to write songs. We wanted to get away from London, and Bernie [Rhodes, The Clash's manager] said me and Mick could go away for two weeks to get the songs, after the tour. He said, 'You can't go to Paris, 'cos you know too many girls there, and you can't go to America.' We were thinking, can't go to Paris, can't go to America, where can we go, ya know? And I said, 'I know Bernie, we'll go to Jamaica!' He goes, 'Fuck off!' Because our manager's very tight, you know, just 'Aw, fuck off!' That's what I expected. And then a couple of weeks later he walks in and he bangs down two tickets to Jamaica. I'd only been joking! And then we thought it was feasible, so me and Mick went. We weren't certain that we wanted to, it was just an idea, but there we were stuck in a hotel.

We wrote about 10 numbers. We ended up just scoring a big bag of grass – we spent all our money on grass – and then we just stayed in our hotel room and smoked it and wrote songs. We ended up there without any money, and you can't go anywhere in Jamaica unless you go by taxi, 'cos there's a lot of gun play and knife play, and if you're white in Jamaica it means you're a rich American. And they don't ask questions. You can't walk about in Kingston, hardly at all, you know.

So we ended up just stuck in a hotel 'cos we couldn't afford it. It was like $10 to ride to the beach. We walked around during the day, to the docks and to score some more. JOE STRUMMER, 1978

If you couldn't find a great photograph down there in 1976 you were blind. God forbid, but it's true. KATE SIMON

Hard to believe these people would become legends. They were just a bunch of people living in the slums trying to make a piece of music or two without any idea that they would ever be internationally renowned. Although they all had pretentions of greatness. They called each other stars. ROGER STEFFENS

In those days it was a competition 'cos everybody wanted to be a superstar, everybody wanted to be the number one. In everything you gotta compete. You gotta strive for what you want, to be better than the next one. But these guys always vibed together. You could see where Bob had that edge though. His mannerisms, charisma; it was all about business. ANTONIO 'GILLIE' GILBERT

We'll never see that again, that musical renaissance period… Of course, kids today will tell you different. They will probably tell you that Donna Summer was putting out better work. DAVID KENNEDY

When I first met Jacob Miller I'd go to his house in Beverly Hills and he'd be in a hammock or, predictably, on the phone. I think Vivien [Goldman] and I are responsible for naming Jacob Miller 'The Killer'.

Jacob and Inner Circle were the heaviest band on the island, mainly due to the fact that they weren't missing many meals... but he was heaven. KATE SIMON

The song 'Wanted' – oh, it's a great tune! Really, really great. And we were there at the time when the elections were kicking off, and Jacob's car got shot up. PAUL SIMONON

Jacob Miller in a cricket outfit? That's chic you know? They were serious about their cricket. KATE SIMON

Three Piece Suit

To see Dillinger, U-Roy and Trinity all together bouncing down the street – to get them all in the frame at the same time – that was a real decisive moment. KATE SIMON

Dillinger (right) had such a profile. It's not surprising he took me shopping for clothes. KATE SIMON

A great picture: the idea that it's 98 degrees out, he's got this woollen cap on and he's not broken a sweat at all. ROGER STEFFENS

And I love his dental work too! In his eyes you can see journalists Neil Spencer and Vivien Goldman. KATE SIMON

When The Clash first started, right, I used to hate reggae.

You know, apart from the early blue beat, I thought it was rubbish, until one day I went to see my mother and there was this thing going through my head: 'House Of Dreadlocks' by Big Youth, you know? And I didn't know what it was and when I got back to London I looked through all the records and I found out it was 'House Of Dreadlocks' by Big Youth and ever since then... suddenly it clicks, right? JOE STRUMMER, 1978

What can I say about Big Youth? Things like *Dread Locks Dread* and *Screaming Target* was such brilliant stuff. What I particularly liked was the dub stuff where there was a lot of harmonica playing. It was absolutely cutting edge. PAUL SIMONON

Bob was definitely listening to Big Youth, he always named Big Youth as one of his favourites and vice versa. RANDALL GRASS

I went to Ras Michael's house one day and I think one of my greatest achievements working in Jamaica was that I was able to smoke a huge spliff, which was mandatory, and then take a great photograph.

I'll tell you something, I got so high that I was confused about what to do with my mortal soul. I said to Ras Michael, 'Is there a place where I can lie down?' So I just went into a room and lay down for a while.

Another time, I asked him, 'When were you born?' and he said, 'I'm born every day.' KATE SIMON

Errol 'T' Brown became the resident sound engineer at Tuff Gong studios in the Eighties. He was the nephew of the legendary Duke Reid, so you could say it was in his genes.

Anyway, he'd completed a highly respectable apprenticeship under Duke, and later with Sonia Pottinger, so he got a lot of work around the island. KATE SIMON

73 DENNIS BROWN

These are great shots of Pablo. The thing about Pablo – and this is where he's similar to Bob Marley – he was always about music, always working on the music. Very serious about it. RANDALL GRASS

That's when we first realised what a melodica was. *East Of The River Nile* and *King Tubby Meets Rockers Uptown* were big hits in London. These were the sort of songs that were played in the punk clubs. PAUL SIMONON

You can't imitate Augustus Pablo. Pablo terrible, man! Pablo heavy. Pablo mean musician, believe me. JUNIOR DELGADO

This is at Channel One; Augustus Pablo with Dennis Brown drinking roots in the background. I've always liked this picture. KATE SIMON

Everybody loved Tubby. He mixed for everybody; he built most of the sound system speakers in Jamaica; he invented dub. They loved him but he was murdered! ROGER STEFFENS

What he had in his filing cabinet, as opposed to files, was a foldable gold crown, and so he obliged me by taking it out and wearing it. KATE SIMON

Legendary drummer; Bob Marley drummer; my brother. That tape machine, I have it at home in my music room. I keep it. It don't play for quite a while but it's good, that Sony tape. Carly come up with it and play that cassette demo tape over in the morning; conga drums and t'ings. ASTON 'FAMILY MAN' BARRETT

If people wanted to talk to you they'd just show up and talk to you in person. There were just a few centres of musical activity. People checked out these places like Channel One and Tommy Cowan's place and then maybe you'd meet somebody there like Inner Circle.

I took a whole bunch of pictures at Dynamics, like the one of Carly and Sly.

I like this picture too because it's the master and the student: Family Man and Robbie Shakespeare. KATE SIMON

That's the legendary producer Bunny 'Striker' Lee stood in between Robbie Shakespeare and Family Man. KATE SIMON

Sly used to work for me man, most a time when it not my machine drum it had Sly. Or me work like a free mason. When them gone we dub with my drummer on my personal drum set and everything into my computer. Black Ark music was in computer from the very beginning. LEE 'SCRATCH' PERRY

Sly was around for long time. He used to play drum all the time before he even come. Him used to play with Ranchie McLean; him used to play with The Revolutionaries; and him used to play a bar club named Tit For Tat on Redhills Road. JUNIOR DELGADO

The thing about Toots Hibbert is, he's really got soul – 'Reggae Got Soul'. STEVE JORDAN

I played on 'Reggae Got Soul' by Toots [and The Maytals]. In fact that was the first song I played reggae on and I think Blackwell was kinda trying me out. Then he sent me on the road with The Heptones and things worked; he figured I was a cool guy so he gave me a job with The Wailers. JUNIOR MARVIN

In the early Seventies, Bob and Toots were about equal popular. In fact, I remember a radio station doing a vote on which one was more popular. I can't remember who won, but it was a close thing.

Toots is an incredible artist, and a lot of those other artists, if they'd had a bit more success could have produced good bodies of work. Toots has been incredible. If he had a band like Bob's that could help write for him, was managed and handled properly, then he could have been really big. DICKIE JOBSON

CULTURE **80**

To me, Culture are the greatest roots harmony group. The *Two Sevens Clash* album is one of the all-time reggae classics. Joseph Hill is kind of a genius; he could actually record a Culture album all by himself. He can sing all the parts and it'll sound like Culture. Great writer, tremendous feeling.
RANDALL GRASS

I love the shot of them at Maypen underneath the television with the roof in the town square. It was the only TV in town.

They were characters, great fun. I took Joseph Hill's picture with Bob Marley at the One Love Peace Concert and I sent him a copy of it. I think Bob was his hero. KATE SIMON

Spear was a country person, he was not a city person, and he had a whole different way of relating to things and expressing himself. It was almost childlike at times. A very gentle person to meet. ROGER STEFFENS

Spear's voice is otherworldly. KATE SIMON

He's very deep. Hypnotic. Very spiritual. There's no type of show or entertainment at all to him. Bob Marley's a showman compared to Spear. Spear just basically chants his music and takes it deeper and deeper, into a hypnotic trance. RANDALL GRASS

The shot of Burning Spear playing football was taken at the Marcus Garvey Youth Club. It was right out on the edge of the sea. He established that for the kids. KATE SIMON

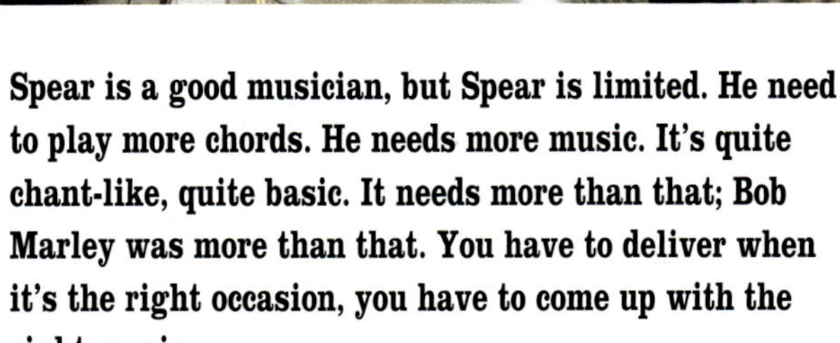

Spear is a good musician, but Spear is limited. He need to play more chords. He needs more music. It's quite chant-like, quite basic. It needs more than that; Bob Marley was more than that. You have to deliver when it's the right occasion, you have to come up with the right music.

Spear is big, but him could be bigger. I just feel it's because he's not coming up with variations of music, which is what music should be. JUNIOR DELGADO

I appreciated Marley and The Wailers big time, but there were other guys, like Burning Spear, who were more extreme maybe, to the point where it was an education in itself trying to work out what the songs were about. Because, culturally, the colour of your skin made a big difference. It wasn't your story. It was about somebody else's oppression. As a white guy living in what may be a poor part of London, there's still no comparison whatsoever to what it's like living in Kingston and the things they had to deal with there. PAUL SIMONON

I was friends with John Lydon. I think he'd just broken up with The Sex Pistols and he was in Jamaica looking for new talent on behalf of Virgin Records. We went to Hellshire beach with U-Roy. John bought a straw hat that he wore all the time, even while swimming.

One time John and I were driving back from the beach or somewhere, and two policemen stopped us with these silver rifles; pewter-coloured muskets, aimed right at us. They said, 'What do you have in your bag?' I should have been more freaked out about it, but I kind of held it together. I said 'Well what I have in here is nothing, I just have a flash gun.' That's not a word you should use in these situations! I had never had a big rifle pointed right in my face. I can't remember John's reaction. We were both just really, really quiet. KATE SIMON

I went with John on that trip. That was the first time I'd been to Jamaica. John took me along because I was black and Jamaican (well sort of). In reality, the closest I'd been to JA was watching *The Harder They Come* in my local movie house in Brixton. Needless to say, sitting around the Sheraton pool with the likes of I-Roy, Big Youth, U-Roy, Prince Far-I, Trinity, The Congos and Tapper Zuckie was pretty impressive to a young Dread from the UK. DON LETTS

85 U-ROY & JOHN LYDON

I'd heard about Countryman from my friend Anna Capaldi; about how this man could catch fish in his bare hands. The first time I met him was at his house at Runaway Bay and the stars were the brightest I've ever seen to this day. All that was on the beach was his shack made of palm trees and palm leaves that rustled in the night breeze.

Elizabeth Barraclough and I were staying in the back of Perry Henzell's place [director and co-writer of *The Harder They Come*] and hanging out with Countryman and Dickie Jobson. Countryman would make us cornmeal porridge for breakfast and magic mushrooms for dinner. He sautéed the mushrooms in butter mind you. A true gourmand, he'd picked them himself and made delicate sandwiches out of them.
KATE SIMON

Countryman was a friend of Bob's friend who had a cottage. Countryman knew the guy who take care of the cottage. But he was a good fisherman, a natureman, understand me? He loved the sea, natural living. He's a good man, a nice guy. ANTONIO 'GILLIE' GILBERT

Bob knew Country and would go to Hellshire occasionally. At first you had to go there by boat because there was no road. He was just a really happy guy. His whole view on life was strange, but interesting. He was living in an ideal situation, on a great beach with all the fish he could eat. He never had any money but... DICKIE JOBSON

They made a movie about him. One time *Rolling Stone* magazine came to Jamaica to do a story on reggae music and the photographer took pictures of Bob and pictures of Country and they actually put Country on the cover! It was like, how did they end up with a picture of a fisherman on the front cover of *Rolling Stone*? WAYNE JOBSON

The piece was written by Michael Thomas and later became a book called *Babylon On A Thin Wire*. It was the article that turned me on to reggae. Changed my whole life, forever. He said: 'Reggae music crawls into your bloodstream like some vampire amoeba from the psychic rapids of upper-Niger consciousness.' I said 'Damn! I don't know what this sounds like but I'm going out right now and I'm going to find some!' I went down to a used record store in Berkeley, where I was living, and found a copy of *Catch A Fire* for two-and-a-quarter, and I didn't take it off the turntable for three weeks. Man, my whole head was blown. I just kept flipping it over. ROGER STEFFENS

I was charmed and intrigued by Chris Blackwell. I felt an easy rapport with him; a friendship developed and he became something of a mentor to me. One of the reasons I believe I got great pictures on the Exodus tour is that it was he who sent me on that tour and I didn't want to disappoint him. True, when I came back I had trouble finding him for six months, but that's Chris.

Next to him is Denise Mills. Wherever Chris went, Denise went. She was his right hand. **KATE SIMON**

Clapton's 'I Shot The Sheriff' was a major event in breaking reggae to a mainstream audience and having people go back to the original, but Chris never deserted the original artists either. He recognised the value of someone like Eric doing a Marley song but we were always going back to the whole spectrum of reggae and Chris was supportive of it all. He had sub labels to release more obscure or less commercial material on.

Being white and British might have helped contribute to some of the bad feeling toward him during that period, but his support and love for the music was unquestionable. A lot of this stuff would never have got out if it weren't for Chris. His taste, his appreciation and his belief in music well beyond its commerciality is well established. **JEFF WALKER**

When a lot of people in the company didn't believe in The Wailers, Chris did. And he was responsible for helping change the songs quite a bit. Like the first album, *Catch A Fire*. Bob had done tracks in Jamaica and then he came over to England and finished mixing them, and a lot of the Island artists of the time played on it. That slide guitar solo on 'Concrete Jungle' wasn't Peter Tosh, it was a guy called Wayne Perkins. And all that stuff on 'Stir It Up' was Rabbit Bundrick.

The other thing they always accuse Chris of is that he broke The Wailers up, which is completely untrue. When Chris started dealing with them he was dealing with Bob Marley. It was always known as Bob Marley and The Wailers, just like Toots and The Maytals and all those other groups. But The Beatles had come in; the American doo-wop thing was looking old-fashioned and yet Jamaican artists were all that way orientated. So, part of the thing was to try and present them as a rock group. So it was, 'Why don't we call them The Wailers?'

They broke up on their own. DICKIE JOBSON

On *Catch A Fire* and *Burnin'*, they're just The Wailers because Bob Marley and The Wailers didn't sound like a group. It sounded like the old-fashioned approach. So I signed Bob Marley and The Wailers but the first two records I put out just as The Wailers. When we had the problem with the other two guys, I went back to Bob Marley and The Wailers. The Wailers became the band.

I think Bob and I had a great working relationship. I think he had a lot of confidence in me because he felt that I knew his music, I knew Jamaican music, and Island at the time we signed him was – I can say it now because I'm looking back 30 years – an incredible company. It was probably one of the hottest labels in the world. So I think he went along with my vision quite happily. I don't think he was nervous about it. I think he really went along with it. In fact, I'm sure he did. CHRIS BLACKWELL

The first time I met Blackwell was at Upsetter's [Lee Perry's] studio. You're talking around 1974 or '75. and he's a man who so humble. Blackwell is a humble lickle, simple lickle man. The reason I say that is I know him from I young and I find him wearing straw hat, short pants and slip-on's, ya know?

Blackwell a god... That man protect them yout' and promote them. Always, Bob Marley music was too hard to promote; it was the man named Blackwell who stand up with it and take all the embarrassment. If a man sing a song 'bout 'Feel like bombing a church/Now that I know the preacher is lying,' how you going to promote that? And Chris Blackwell take it and promote it. It not only fe Bob Marley him doing that. Him do the same job if any man come with a good product; he take it and get fully behind it. A whole heap a'other groups he work with and bust them big time.

But them don't give him his due. That's how they treat a humble man, all the time. 'Cos Blackwell is a humble man, ya know? And he was a successful guy. Him have the magic. Whatever he touch turns to gold.

If I'm doing something and it is successful how you gonna hate me? That mean you gonna hate success. Somewhere you are wrong.

Blackwell is a blessed man and Bob Marley did love him. And I have to love Blackwell too because he was the only man who prove that reggae music can be as big as any other music. Don't think Blackwell don't go through embarrassment. When he heard Four Tops, Smokey Robinson and all these groups, people were saying reggae finished because it doesn't have all these strings and all of this.

It's not only him. You have to give thanks to Coxsone too, Beverley's [Leslie Kong's label] and Duke Reid; you have to give thanks to all of them. But Blackwell is the man who take this to the world. JUNIOR DELGADO

20
BOB M
THE W

00
ARLEY
AILERS

EXODUS

Following the success of 1975's *Live!*, the following year *Rastaman Vibration* was released. Mellower in mood and with Neville Garrick's distinctive hessian cloth packaging, it finally broke the American market reaching Number Eight on the US charts. This confirmed Bob as a serious star and the ears of the world were now attuned to Jamaica.

Bob had also become a target for the British tabloid press, thanks partly to his relationship with the then Miss World, Cindy Breakspeare.

He'd been living in London since late 1976 having fled Jamaica following an assassination attempt. Smile Jamaica, an enormous free concert featuring the best artists in the country, had effectively been hijacked by Prime Minister Michael Manley in an attempt to get re-elected.

Whether the political overtones of the forthcoming event had anything to do with the gunmen breaking through the gate of 56 Hope Road on 3 December, 1976, spraying bullets indiscriminately, has long been the subject of debate. Rita Marley was shot in the head; Don Taylor, Bob's manager, was shot five times in the groin; Bob himself narrowly escaped serious injury, flattening himself against a wall. Still, a bullet grazed his chest and lodged in his arm.

Amazingly, no one was killed - though Don Taylor only just survived - and a mere 48 hours later Bob and Rita appeared at the concert. In the final number, Bob defiantly showed his wounds to the crowd.

Immediately after, he boarded a plane to Nassau, before moving on to London. It was there, while living on Oakley Street in the relatively plush area of Chelsea, that Bob wrote and recorded what many consider his masterpiece: *Exodus*.

I was lucky enough to visit a few times, and by this time he was a massive star. The shooting had conferred upon him almost martyr status.

My intuition was that Bob was on the way to attaining a level of global influence, that the message of his music was going to be felt all over the world.

So I didn't have to think long when Chris Blackwell asked me to follow the band on their 1977 European tour.

I had just moved to New York and my studio was right across the street from Chris' place at Essex House, so he and I flew to Paris together. To celebrate the beginning of the Exodus tour, there was a huge party at the Elysées Matignon in Paris. Johnny Halliday, Ahmet Ertegun, Bianca Jagger - all the celebrities of the day were there. The Rastas were all sitting at one table and Bob was dancing. Paris was never the same... KATE SIMON

The tour was a great success culminating in some incendiary shows at London's Rainbow Theatre that were filmed for a live video. After Europe, the band were due to continue their tour in the US. By this point, however, Bob was beginning to feel the full effect of a football injury received before the first gig in Paris. During a game against a team of French journalists, an opposing player stood on his foot. With the toenail bruised and bloody, he was taken to hospital where doctors first noticed what they thought was a melanoma.

The tour continued, and so did the games of football, albeit with sandals, bandages and a padded toecap. But while the simple soccer injury healed, what the doctors had uncovered would later claim his life.

At that time I'd just left school and I was working a lot with Traffic; Chris Wood, Steve Winwood, Jim Capaldi and all those people. They were the ones who actually got me into The Wailers because I'd played on *Arc Of A Diver*, a Steve Winwood solo album, and Chris Blackwell heard it and thought the guitar playing was Steve. He said, 'Steve, the guitar playing's really cool, it's brilliant.' And he said, 'Oh no, it's this little Jamaican guy who does it for me.' So he came hunting for me and the next thing I knew Chris took me to Bob and said, 'Hey, you don't even need to audition, you're in The Wailers.' I'm like, 'Wait a minute, hold on!' Funnily enough, in that same week I got a call from Stevie Wonder to join his band, so it was a crazy week for me. What I eventually did was let my friends decide. I said, 'You guys choose for me, I can't choose.' They said, 'Bob Marley's your countryman, you need to go with your countryman.' So I did. JUNIOR MARVIN

We went from Paris to Brussels, to The Hague, to Munich, to Heidelberg, then Hamburg and Berlin – Bob did an incredible rendition of 'War' in Berlin, really incredible – then we went to Stockholm, Copenhagen, Gothenburg and on to London for those famous four nights at the Rainbow.

It was the courage of the young because I was all alone. I had one suitcase for my cameras, one for my clothing, one for my camera accoutrements; it's a lot of stuff. I remember walking across the street to meet Chris and go to Paris and feeling a combination of... I wasn't afraid, I just felt: 'Woah, this is going to be a hell of a ride!' KATE SIMON

I liked her photographs and she had a sort of war correspondent feel to her; she would get right into it. She travelled the whole way on the bus with them, roughed it up with everybody; she was really ready to do that and somehow she had the ability to communicate and to get everybody to relax and take the great pictures that she got.

I just wanted to try and capture that whole sense of what a tour was all about. What it was like with these guys travelling through very foreign worlds as a group; like a band of gypsies almost. I wanted to capture that. CHRIS BLACKWELL

Yes, she was a good person and she was touring with us as our photographer. She was sent on a mission to prove something, just to have some photos; to get some good pictures of The Wailers. ASTON 'FAMILY MAN' BARRETT

1977 was when I think Bob really went global. As it came out about his girlfriend Cindy Breakspeare, Bob became a tabloid item. More than just *Melody Maker* and *New Musical Express* and stuff like that, he was now in the *Mirror*, the *Sun* and the *Daily Mail*. They wrote some stupid stuff though, calling him the 'wild man of reggae'! And some articles said things like Cindy had married the 'Prince of Wails'. That really broke out around the Exodus tour, the same tour he hurt his toe in Paris playing a football game. NEVILLE GARRICK

It was fun, ya know? And work! It was no joke, it was work. You gotta be on it man. It was just timing; Bob wasn't a guy that don't keep up to his appointments. He was always on time for shows, always on time for interviews. He was disciplined like that. He was dedicated, committed to what he was doing. ANTONIO 'GILLIE' GILBERT

At that time we would have in-house people who we'd put on different projects: roadies, tour managers, guys that hauled the equipment. But the main thing is that Bob had this way so that people loved him. The people who worked for him, they loved him. He wasn't all over them and he wasn't patting them on the back, but there was something about him. There was a warmth to him. Even though he wasn't communicating it all of the time there was a kind of aura about him. Probably the short answer to why they liked working for him is that he led by example. The stars of most shows turn up 20 minutes late, crack a joke, everybody laughs and off they go. Bob was the first person on the bus. He would be sitting there and waiting for everybody to come and so he helped those people do their jobs. If he was the first there, there was no excuse for anybody else not to be there. That was the really unique thing about Bob: he never differentiated himself from anybody. He never played the star. I'd say he was just a natural leader. He didn't have to shout, he didn't have to scream, he just commanded that kind of respect. CHRIS BLACKWELL

DIO
D I O
EXECUTIVES LTD.

I don't have time to fight. If I fight, I hurt myself. I leave the judgement to God. The rocks in a river never prevented the water from flowing. BOB MARLEY, 1980

He was the first one on the bus. There was never any, 'I travel separately.' I think he really lived as if we were all inter-dependent and never showed himself in any way to be special. He didn't act like he was a rock star and I sensed that he felt quite uncomfortable with being treated as one. When he'd come into a room after a show and he'd just want to chill out, the whole room would stop and I almost felt sorry for him. But I was very taken with all their behaviour. This was no rock tour, this was something more. It was something totally unique that you would never experience again in your life. Even at the time, 46 years ago, I knew that. KATE SIMON

He got on the tour bus first so he would know who was slacking! We used to call him, affectionately, 'Skipper', 'cos he was like a captain, f'real! NEVILLE GARRICK

He was a hard working man. You ought to see his kids, they share the same ethic. They just work.

You probably know this, but on stage he must sing and do things right. If it go no right, him'll stand and wait 'til the band get the groove. When the band get the groove right, he'd say, alright, all those hours ya spent in rehearsal pay off, we can go out on stage and do it. DAVID KENNEDY

When Bob was living up at Nine Mile, he was growing food. He wasn't making any money from music, and Rita was there. A guy told me that Bob could clear a whole hillside of bush in one day; any other guy it would take them a week to clear the hillside and plant yams, cocoa and potato. Bob could do it in a day. They said he was the hardest worker out of any person. It's that discipline to clear the thing in a whole day when any other guy would come out there and maybe smoke a joint until two, do two hours of work then go and sleep. Bob was there at six o'clock in the morning. It's that kind of discipline that sets him as a great artist. WAYNE JOBSON

That's one thing a lot of artists don't realise about Bob. There is a sort of Bob Marley syndrome among artists who came after him: they want to achieve the same status and fame without the work. Bob was a worker. When he was on stage, it was just like when you go to the office: it was work. When it was time for rehearsal there was no joking. You knew to be there and don't make a mistake. And it's true, Bob was the first one on the bus. First one, not the last. He didn't take the privilege of taking his time. When it was time to work, everything – girls, football, everything – was put to the side. Music, rehearsal, performance; when that was done everything else could happen. He was very much the leader of The Wailers. In my experience, witnessing many moments with all of them, he was clearly the leader. He consulted different people for different things – assistance, advice, lyrical content, music – but without having to establish authority, he was the main authority. DERA TOMPKINS

Neville Garrick doesn't get enough credit for his talent and his art direction. What he did for Bob Marley in his album artwork is nothing short of spectacular. KATE SIMON

Neville was kind of quiet but he did terrific work. He was brought into the circle and the more he became a part of them and lived with them, the more he became part of the family. Particularly in later years and after Bob's passing. JEFF WALKER

I was reading a book called *Dread*. It was a book written about Rastafarians by a Roman Catholic priest of all people. He was actually quite positive. I think one of the influences I had on Bob was encouraging him to read. Coming from being a member of the Black Panther party when I was in the US, I knew a lot about socialist skills in terms of black empowerment and I read a lot about black history. So, he read some of those books. They expanded his world somewhat more outside of Jamaica.

The first backdrop I did was of Marcus Garvey. That was for the first two tours, I think. Then I did one of His Majesty, then a large one of the Ethiopian flag.

But that was the colour that I brought to the table. Because before me, no reggae group really had an art director, or anything like that. It wasn't something that was considered necessary. Having gone to school in California, I brought that experience of the 'show' part of the business. Going to school in Hollywood, I knew that presentation was very important. NEVILLE GARRICK

I was actually recruited to come and work for the *Jamaican Daily News* 'cos I had some tabloid experience running the black students' newspaper at UCLA. Allan 'Skill' Cole came to look me up and ask me to work on a design for Dizzy Moore's album *In A Mellow Mood* and one thing led to another.

While I was at the *Daily News* they did a concert – The Wailers opened for Marvin Gaye – and I went with the newspaper to take photographs. This was the first time I had seen The Wailers since the release of *Catch A Fire* and I was blown away 'cos they blew Marvin Gaye off stage. From then I knew this group was gonna be very special. We did a big spread on the show and eventually my friend, the features editor, decided to do a piece on them. We went to Hope Road and we met with Bob, we met with Bunny and Peter, and we ended up with five pages. So that was my cue; I resigned from the newspaper and kind of went to work for him. Not in an official capacity, but basically hanging around doing labels and stuff. I think I did one of the first posters of Bob in Jamaica, using some of the shots I'd taken at the concert. I showed him and he said, 'OK, let's get the fucker out and sell it in the shop!' That was the deal. The first album cover I was supposed to do was *Natty Dread*, and I went to England with a concept and stuff, but Island Records had their in-house guy, Tony Wright, who did the painting so I didn't get to do that one. I got to do the next one, which was *Rastaman Vibration,* and I officially became his art director. NEVILLE GARRICK

In everything there is good and bad, even in technology. And when the white man is in power, he doesn't want to acknowledge the black man is his brother. Men must learn to live together, in harmony with each other.

All of what the white leaders did has been machine guns and bombs. So, we disqualify them as leaders, or they rather disqualify themselves because they ignore the right way. They still think they must kill to survive. The white man failed to rule the world. Now the black man's time has come. BOB MARLEY, 1980

If you wanna dance then you go dance disco. But if it's something more for the benefit musically, then you gonna listen to the reggae because you have to listen to it as our God make it. He make it up for your interest, it no gonna trick you.

The more reggae them play, the more Rasta they have. The more the yout' listen. So if we play more disco, then we will have more eyebrow pencils and lipsticks, hear me? The more reggae ya play, the more roots. The more disco you play, the more fantasy ya get. I'm gonna think about the glass, with the wine in it, and that pretty girl with that car park outside, and take a few drinks and go out... so 'im all go try live the rich life and dem is never get it. You gotta check the psychology behind everything. Why is this, why is that? BOB MARLEY, 1979

I started touring with him in 1975, the Natty Dread tour. Since then I think I've seen Bob play live more than anyone else 'cos I was the art director and the lighting director, so I was always out front. I saw over 500 concerts like that. Every night it was a new concert; I never got bored. When I started we were playing for 400 or 500 people and in the end we were doing stadiums of 100,000 in Milan. Going through that was a great experience and a great privilege.

Hanging around him you were encouraged to get involved. So I ended up playing percussion whenever there were daytime shows I couldn't light. Because, when we were recording, so many people played percussion on the recording Seeco couldn't play all those different parts himself. So, by going up there I could add some of the few little beats that Seeco couldn't catch. But that was due to his encouragement; he figured if I got more involved that way, then my interpretation of the music would be more. NEVILLE GARRICK

**A cry of the human spirit, an expression of joyousness.
A celebration of being alive and saying 'I'm here!'** RANDALL GRASS

Neville Garrick did a beautiful light show. He used a lot of gold light. I knew where he was coming from and that he wanted to keep the lights low. For me, as a photographer, it wasn't the easiest light to work with but, because I prefer available light, I would shoot handheld. It was quite a challenge. KATE SIMON

I probably couldn't light anyone else because I knew every single beat. And lighting, half of it is anticipation: if you don't track on the beat then it doesn't have the effect. If it comes before or after then it's not the same. I usually say I coloured the music, that was my job! NEVILLE GARRICK

HE OFTEN SEEMED TO HAVE A KIND OF MELANCHOLY ABOUT HIM.
HE WAS SERIOUS, PENSIVE. KATE SIMON

That man have the blues, ya know? Bob Marley, full up of the blues.
And it's the same music, just played in a different way. JUNIOR DELGADO

Let me tell you something 'bout me. Me grew in a suffering and I don't know how to live good, I only know how to suffer, y'unnerstahn? I don't really think my life that God make me live through as a sin. That's the way I want me to stay. What is big life to some people? That is not what I call life. What me call life is when I wake up and get a lickle bush tea. And survive. But I don't really know about the big life.

BOB MARLEY, 1980

THE WAILERS

That's a shamanistic picture. That's not someone who's concerned about whether he's looking nice for the first row. It wasn't a performance, it was more a transcendental experience for him. He was more shaman than showman. RANDALL GRASS

Woah! What kind a' clothes he got on man? Must have been cold. DAVID KENNEDY

It was May in Europe, and he was always carrying his parka with him, his anorak. He was terrified of being cold I think. I have so many pictures of him in the height of spring, looking at June, and he's carrying his parka with him. KATE SIMON

Coca-Cola

I always want to get as much eye contact with the subject as possible. I look for that.

He worked with me and it really broadened me as a photographer. So, I experimented. I took more colour than I had ever taken before and bounced flash in ways I'd never done before. Bob Marley helped me and that's all part of his generosity.

The photo opposite was taken at 52 Oakley Street [the house he and the band lived in when in London] the night before he opened at the Rainbow. KATE SIMON

It was like, wherever Bob was, you wanted to be. Sometimes he'd fall asleep on the floor. There'd be all sorts of people there visiting, talking and stuff and everybody would fall asleep on the floor. He'd wake up in the morning and they'd have cleaned the fridge out and there'd be nothing left for us. JUNIOR MARVIN

Record company no realise, this music can unify the whole universe. The truth that the music carry and the whole philosophy, the ideology behind it – record company no idea of that. Record company need a record make it on the charts.
BOB MARLEY, 1979

Gillie would dance on the side of the stage like no one you've ever seen in your life. He was like an Arabian knight, skanking. He would drive the audience. He was part of the show, believe me! KATE SIMON

Every concert I vibe it, ya know? ANTONIO 'GILLIE' GILBERT

I was Bob's bredren. We met because of Rasta vibes, the Rastafari connection; the conscious vibe of The Wailers at the time. Because it wasn't just Bob, it was The Wailing Wailers at the time. I met the group as a young kid going to school. That was my group. You know how you idolise a group? That was my group, The Wailing Wailers.

We become friends because after school I always go to this joint where we burn; we smoke and vibe together. It was just a natural vibe. They playing their guitar, we're there supporting them, I wouldn't say as fans, but as bredren and bredren, vibing.

He always wanted me to go on tour with him but I would do my own thing. Over the years we've been vibing in Jamaica, it so 'appen that they were going on tour in '77 so I decided to make that move. They'd been touring from early '73, '74, '75 when they were just gaining ground, building, so at that time they didn't have that money to have support staff like a cook or whatever.

As the years go by, he grew, and you can see the improvements every year. That's what I admired about him: every year he was improving. ANTONIO 'GILLIE' GILBERT

We always took our own cook on tour with us to make sure that we had a proper diet and nobody on the road would get sick eating things like fast food. So we'd bring a pot of Jamaican stuff with us. When we were first in England it used to be Carly the drummer who'd cook, until Gillie came a couple of months later. Gillie was a great cook. And he was also a great soccer player. NEVILLE GARRICK

Gillie's a good football player, not such a good cook. He used to heap Bob's food up like a mountain, Bob would sit there 'n say, 'It don' even look pretty!' Instead of putting a bit of salad on the side and a lickle rice here, he'd just mash it all together. Gillie was there to play football. Without a doubt. And for everything else you're not supposed to do that Jamaicans do that's illegal. JUNIOR MARVIN

That's 'cos he was a punk. In those days, Junior wasn't a vegetarian. He had a totally different mentality. He was a Londoner. He wasn't used to good, natural food. ANTONIO 'GILLIE' GILBERT

He's a gentle spirit. DERA TOMPKINS

Gillie

GILLIE'S RECIPE FOR IRISH MOSS:

Irish moss from the bottom of the sea [seaweed].

Clean it first, wash it good; sometime just boil it then dry it.

Add a little water, boil it for a certain amount of time and add linseed, flaxweed and stuff like gum arabic and isinglass that stabilise the moss.

Boil it down to a nice simmer then it thick up and your common sense says it boil and ready.

Strain it and sweeten it with honey or a little milk, and then you drink it.

Ital food you pick off the tree, you pull it up out of the ground, or you go get a handful of it out of the sea. That's ital food. You've got the sea moss, Irish moss, cooked without the money that buys salt, the money that buys pepper or the money that buys seasoning. It's ital because it's cooked with all the ingredients from the earth.
DANNY SIMS

We make all kind of stuff. Good Jamaican stuff, vegetarian. Ital stew, a lot of juices; different types of juices we blend and put together. It's just a variety of good stuff. A combination of ingredients.

In the morning, Bob really loved his bush tea; things like mint tea and fever grass, all the good herbs in Jamaica, mixed into a blend of two or three. He'd drink a tea first and then eat fruit, like suck two orange. And then we go jog, 'cos you can't jog with full belly. Then after he have good Irish moss and good porridge. Then we cook down the vegetables. We always have things stirring. The fire always keep burning with food; bowl of fish tea, big pot of Irish moss. We cook down some steam fish, or fry down some fish, or cook down the good ital stew. In that we'd put the best in vegetables, red bean, coconut milk, carrot, turnip, pumpkin; whatever was in season at the time. ANTONIO 'GILLIE' GILBERT

Ital comes from the word 'vital'. It is a natural diet. I guess it wasn't founded by the Rastas but a lot of it is provided by the Bible and a lot of it is just good common sense in terms of what is good for us and what is healthy. It can be very thick; no salt, no sugar, no canned goods, all fresh foods. What they say is 'no deadas'. Nothing that's dead. Shellfish and pork are items that many Rastas don't eat. Some houses of Rasta will eat chicken, goat and beef. Some will eat no fish and are total vegetarians. The house of Rasta you're in, or the community you're part of, dictates what your dietary restrictions might be. But mostly they are healthy eaters. Food is fresh everyday. People who lived in the hills, they didn't have refrigerators so everyday they went to market to buy food so that people ate fresh vegetables and healthy food, three meals a day. DERA TOMPKINS

EXECUTED
DAILY EXPRESS
DROGERIE
SOUVENIRS
PEPSI
Lufthansa

We love to read paper, news, ya know? Although me is not a man from the university, but I can read the news. I can read the news and understand I-self. I can write songs, say things as they should be said. JUNIOR DELGADO

That's another interesting thing about reggae: it's like a musical newspaper. It's talking about what affects the people. It's about personal mindsets. It's about humans and what they have to suffer, rather than just: I love you, you love me... or whatever. It's about personal politics, which later became very important for The Clash. PAUL SIMONON

Mainly they travelled by bus but then there would be a lot of these little planes too and every time the plane landed somebody would yell out, 'Jah Rastafari!' I don't think they liked flying very much. KATE SIMON

A lot of Rastas do not trust what they call the iron bird. DERA TOMPKINS

The shot opposite, I love. I'm printing it for the first time. I think it says a lot because Bob used to fly alone; there wouldn't be someone sitting next to him. And he would always take his guitar on the plane with him. KATE SIMON

FRAGILE
FRAGILE
CHICAGO GUITAR GALLERY

Do you hear that? Now, that's night. That's really the music I listen to: crickets, frogs, the sounds of nature. If you go to the countryside with a tape recorder, you find the music of the hills. It's different from commercial music. Once you record, that's commerce, that's 'bizniz'. Music is the chant of the earth. If you listen to it, nature is music, and music is there for changes. It brings the strength of the rhythm to the people. BOB MARLEY, 1980

Seeco wrote 'Work'. He was coming into a rehearsal, counting off the miles as he was writing it – five miles to go – and he sang it for Bob and Bob said, 'I like that song and I'm going to record it, but we'll change the miles to days.' So Bob counted off the last days of his life in the last song he ever sang live, as a medley with 'Get Up, Stand Up'. ROGER STEFFENS

Seeco knew Bob from down in Trench Town. Bob really liked him, though he was a really quiet guy. He was there from the first tour. When he first arrived he didn't fit the image of the band at all; here was a very young rock group from Jamaica and Seeco looked a bit old. DICKIE JOBSON

On the planes nobody said anything to me except Seeco. He presumed that I didn't like to fly, which wasn't true at the time; I didn't care. Anyway, Seeco would come over to me and put these earphones on me playing 'Stardust', the Hoagy Carmichael song. I like Seeco so much. KATE SIMON

I was wondering, when I went on that European tour, did he know that he had cancer? Because from what I understood, in May '77 he had the accident with the French soccer player then he found out it was cancerous in July, so does that mean when I was on the tour with him in May he didn't know it was cancer? I was aware that he was injured, not because of the way he walked or anything but because he'd wear sandals during the day and he had a significant bandage on his toe. Then at night he'd do an unbelievable show and he was wearing these zipped up boots and jumping around and everything.

I never talked about it to him, and I never heard the band talking about it. I have that picture of him laughing, smiling on the bus and that foot bandaged, held up in the air.

I don't know enough about Rastafari and his spiritual beliefs, but I suspect that he had turned it over and put it in God's hands. KATE SIMON

It didn't look serious when he first did it, but after the doctors did all kind of stuff with him, that's when everything went crazy. I wasn't there at the time, because we had to finish the game. When the game was finished and we went to the hotel, they brought him back with bandages on his toes, and... you can see here he had a smashed toe. This was just the beginning of the tour, and he toured with sandals and worked out the tour. When the tour was finished, the toe got better. I think when he came to the States, he injured it again. He had to take care of some business in London, so he went back to London and decided to examine the foot properly again and that's when they came up with this idea it's cancerous. They told him he had to cut off the toe, so that's when things started getting crazy. A little panic, but not much. He was kinda nervous so he flew back here and they got a specialist to look at it. They did some stuff to it and it got better. They say if you've got a wound and it's cancerous it can't heal, and this one healed. It was healing up and everything was fine. In Paris, they took the nail out at the root, which I think they shouldn't have done. When he was playing soccer, he had to put a cap over his toe, like a cushion. And he played soccer hard, same way. Everything was fine. And a couple years after they're saying that he had cancer, from the toe, all up. It's crazy. They took the life away but the spirit still live. It's like prophecy; you see Bob's face all over the world now. They can't get him out of the race.
ANTONIO 'GILLIE' GILBERT

PEOPLE OF

This was the band celebrating Seeco's birthday after the show in Heidelberg, Germany. There was a great feeling on the tour. It was like an invisible force field was surrounding them. KATE SIMON

There was always a good atmosphere on tour with Bob. You always felt good in a room with him and all the band. It was probably all the ganja they were smoking. SPENCER DAVIS

Sometimes guys have personal problems and whatever, but 95 per cent it was all good. I ain't gonna say 100 per cent; some guys get on the road and things get out of proportion, but they got control, you know? Because you can't afford to mess with the movement. You can't have no blemishes on the movement. It was just positive vibes. ANTONIO 'GILLIE' GILBERT

He was really sweet around the fans. These pictures were taken in Stockholm; he was signing autographs. KATE SIMON

What a lot of people don't know is that Bob loved children. He worshipped them. I remember taking my son backstage once – he must have been about nine years old – Bob went straight to him and spent all his time talking to him and ignoring me. His eyes would light up when he saw kids. SPENCER DAVIS

I didn't talk casually to him. At the live shows I was right in front of him. I was on the bus, at all the sound checks and when he'd go to the park I'd trail them; but I was always welcome. He must have respected that I was working hard because he was a hard worker himself.

Gillie and Bob and Seeco and Rita and everybody were all in the hotel playing around and playing football and there were times when I'd hang out with them. But people agree: Bob didn't have a tendency towards small talk and I certainly experienced that. He seemed to be very intuitive and almost psychic. I felt he was talking to me by giving me such great photographs. He never once said to me, 'You can't participate in this situation, go away.' KATE SIMON

Bob Marley was one of the greatest prophets we've heard in modern times. He loved yout's. I can remember a lickle yout' who Bob Marley love, from lower Trench Town who used to cook fe him. And there was yout' like me. Bob Marley never had fe love all these yout's and all these people who queued to get a pot on the fire, or something to drink to quench their thirst. So, he was a blessed man. JUNIOR DELGADO

Carly

BOB MARLEY & THE WAILERS

The earlier shows I remember, he would start with his back to the audience and he would just play the tune; just keep playing the instrumental of it until the band locked. He'd play with his back to the audience and then when the band were finally playing right he'd turn around and start to sing. I think that says a lot. He wasn't all show business. It needed to lock into place before he really felt it and got going. CHRIS BLACKWELL

I kinda go into a bit of a trance when I play. I don't really think about what I'm gonna play next; I let it come through me, the energy. After you rehearse then it becomes subconscious because you've been through the mechanics so many times. If you can't play it by then you shouldn't be on the stage. You can let go and just let it happen. We would have a song arranged but Bob might do something and we could follow him because we knew it that well. He'd have cues that he would make to us that the audience would never pick up. With Family Man and Carly we also had a very solid base. We were very, very confident because everyone knew each other's parts. The fact that we rehearsed so much meant you got to know your part inside out. JUNIOR MARVIN

Bob Marley was an entertainer. If you call Michael Jackson an entertainer because he's a great dancer, his dynamics in dancing were no more dynamic than Bob's moves on stage. You're talking about two of the greatest entertainers of all time in concert. Bob Marley was not just a revolutionary poet – and one of the greatest – but he was entertaining too. In his way, he was one of the greatest entertainers I have ever seen. His performances were all the same; from playing the guitar in front of a small audience in a high school in London, to playing on a big stage, that electricity was there. Whether it was a cappella or whether it was with his band. DANNY SIMS

The concerts were mind blowing. You shivered. You got goosebumps just to see the audience. And the attendance was unbelievable. Knowing it's Bob Marley coming from a third world country and having that power. It's not just white folks or black folks, it's all nations zooming in on this vibe. So this is a good vibe! It's a positive vibration, as he said. And it was for the people; he said music is for the people. We hear music and we feel no pain. He was trying to get the message across to the world: unity, togetherness, love, sharing, caring. But I guess the world wasn't seeing that. I mean, just like what's happening now... all this craziness happening.

And we knew everything that was gonna happen. As Rastas, we've studied this; we've known t'ings like this is gonna happen and there's a lot more to happen. As Bob said: 'There's a natural mystic blowing through the air.' He said, 'Many more will have to suffer/Many more will have to die/Don't ask me why.' ANTONIO 'GILLIE' GILBERT

He had tremendous respect for his audience. In fact, each town we went to he'd want to find out what were their favourite songs, and he would actually play them. Because I would kinda do that research when we were on the road. They loved 'Three Little Birds', and there were standards like 'Get Up, Stand Up', and 'No Woman No Cry'. After those songs were established they would be on every set.

There was one concert we did in Oslo, Norway, where it was raining from before we got there and was still raining when we left the next day, and that's the longest concert I think Bob ever did. He performed for about three hours and ran out of songs 'cos he wouldn't perform anything he hadn't rehearsed. But that tour was a big thing. We literally prepared for about two months before going on it by jogging, running, rehearsing... I've never seen no musicians so dedicated to their performance. He really, really worked for it. NEVILLE GARRICK

It's amazing: you'd go to a concert with Bob Marley and the people in the audience after his show would be in a daze. I mean, they would be on a high. Even if a guy didn't feel good and he went to a Bob Marley concert he would end up energised. Every time I saw a show I was energised. DANNY SIMS

We'd talk about everything. Part of the music was not just playing but talking. Half of it was talking about it, the other half was actually playing. So, we'd have meetings to discuss who needed to tighten up or who needed to learn what, how we could develop or what different signals meant, so that we'd all be on the same page. It was pretty tight, but it was a lot of fun too. It wasn't always super serious; as you can see, Bob's laughing in a lot of pictures. There was always somebody cracking a joke. As well as the serious side to him there was a lot of humour as well. He wasn't Mr Serious all the time, thinking about the state of the world. He was pretty jovial. Jamaicans love to joke, though nobody else understands their jokes! It was pretty good vibes.

And you can see, we were always jamming; in the dressing room, every chance that we got. Top left has Tyrone on bass, Family Man playing, like, table drums, Carly just looking in. We were always playing and always together. JUNIOR MARVIN

Family
Man

Tyrone made a living from playing in a hotel band over in Ocho Rios. During the winter, at the weekends or on their days off, he'd go to Kingston and record with Bob. It was a big thing 'cos who wants to play in a stupid hotel band where you're playing 'Yellow Bird' and 'This Is My Island In The Sun'? You want to play good stuff, but tourists don't wanna hear that. So you play there, you make a living, then you go to Kingston, play on Bob's records.

He goes one time on his day off, plays, and when he gets back to the hotel, the bandleader says, 'I understand that you were in Kingston recording a session...' And he say, 'Yes, I was playing with Bob Marley,' expecting the guy to say, 'Wow!' The guy says, 'Oh, so you leave my work and go to play with those dirty Rastas? You're fired.' He got fired for recording with Bob. Now can you think of any more of a class system than that? Instead of being rated and respected for recording with Bob Marley, he gets fired from the hotel band because he played with dirty Rastas. WAYNE JOBSON

153 TYRONE DOWNIE

Backstage, you might think Bob would have a private room. Oh no! He was there with his people. And to be backstage, talk about energy! There were all sorts of people, there was music and food... it was an experience. Or to be in the hotel, or to be on the bus... There was a movement of Jah people and he did his part, he did it well. He deserved his rest. DERA TOMPKINS

He really had very little privacy, especially on tour. He had this massive entourage, basically all kinds of hangers on. I would be interviewing him and I'd show up at the hotel room and there'd be all these people there. With Bob it was basically like Jesus and his disciples, and it'd be a reasoning session. RANDALL GRASS

I can't be sure but I think Neville Garrick took this shot of Bob and me. Whoever it was, I'm glad that they did because it's the only one I have. KATE SIMON

I can't remember taking that shot at all! NEVILLE GARRICK

I like this: 'You're asking the wrong questions...' STEVE JORDAN

Look at the vex on him there... Feel it! Man, he don't like the interview, serious t'ing. That man'll tell you the truth. He's a truthful man, Bob Marley. That's why you had certain people at the time – certain journalists and people in high places – never like him. Because he's licking out and he's speaking the truth. JUNIOR DELGADO

Rico Rodriguez, the great trombonist, opened for Bob on the Exodus tour. He was a graduate of the famed Alpha Boys' School that turned out virtually all the best Jamaican horn players, including Don Drummond and Tommy McCook. KATE SIMON

Around this time was when we first made real contact with the Ethiopian Royal Family. The Crown Prince Asfa Wossen was living in London and we got to meet him. That's when Bob got his Lion of Judah ring. NEVILLE GARRICK

This shot was taken in London. There was an Ethiopian fundraising function going on. Bob gave them a whole bunch of money. Bob was very, very generous; he'd always give money to people who needed it. JUNIOR MARVIN

This is an amazing picture. Look at all that love! It's beautiful, just beautiful. STEVE JORDAN

Colin Lesley – who ran Tuff Gong for him and was his accountant as well – was the man who had to co-sign the cheques or they weren't valid. So, no one knew how Bob spent his money the way Colin understood how. I asked Colin if it were true that Bob really supported 4,000 people, and he shook his head and he said, 'No, no, much more than that.' He wagers around 6,000 people, each month, depended on their support directly from Bob Marley. Six thousand people. He was selfless, he gave almost all his money away. He bought houses for all kinds of people: members of the band, Judy, Junior, relatives, his mother, cousins, aunts, uncles. Never had a house of his own, really. He had a room at his mother's in Miami, had a cot upstairs in Tuff Gong for a long time, and then the last 18 months of his life he finally got a bed. Some of the women in his life made him buy a bed. He was just as happy sleeping on the ground with that fabled rock stone for a pillow. He was a country boy. If interviewers asked him what he was, he would say, 'I'm a farmer.' Because he came from the country, he was a farmer. And he went back to it a couple of times when he tried to quit the business. Very humble guy in many ways. ROGER STEFFENS

He would feed the world. Black, white, any kind of man, him no partial. People would line up, queue up to get money, school clothes, anything that could help a family, he would give it to them. Rude boy get things for family. Bad boy come look food and get food from him. Bob Marley a god, man. JUNIOR DELGADO

This was taken after a performance in Berlin. I gave Rita a print of it as a condolence gift, in Kingston, the day before Bob's funeral. KATE SIMON

He was a rhythm guitarist. Him could hold his own and write his songs, but he wasn't a guitar player to go up there and play other people's stuff. But he was good doing his own thing and writing his own stuff. JUNIOR DELGADO

I used to have to give him lessons everyday. Because Chris Blackwell said I had to show him a few things so he can get better and better, and Bob wasn't really a lead player so I just showed him some lead stuff. I gave him a few ideas; I gave him the idea for 'Could You Be Loved'. I played this guitar lick... Da Na Na Na, Da Da Da Da... And the next morning he comes up and sings: 'Could you be loved/And be loved...' I said, 'Shit! You gotta gimme some royalties!' He just laughed. The thing is, the way he gave royalties was like, when the money came in he'd give me a little extra, which he wouldn't tell anyone else about. That was the way he operated, you know? I guess, after going through hell with Peter and Bunny he was reluctant to sign things with people. But he ended up playing really good rhythm guitar. Excellent rhythm guitar. JUNIOR MARVIN

It was more the guitar playing of a songwriter than a guitar player if you know what I mean. Peter had a more distinctive guitar sound in the way of getting that little scratch, and he was a stronger guitarist. Bob's guitar was much more an instrument on which to write; a base from which to write a song. CHRIS BLACKWELL

I remember when they came back from that very first British tour with Peter and Bunny. He came back to Jamaica and I said, 'Well, what was the tour like?' And he said, 'I can't believe people were cheering me; it was the first time I ever held a guitar on stage!' He thought he was up there playing terribly and the people were cheering; but of course they weren't necessarily cheering the guitar playing, they were cheering him. WAYNE JOBSON

He didn't really consider himself to be a great guitarist. But I remember that brown guitar [Gibson Les Paul Special, opposite]; when he bought it he said he wouldn't take it on stage until he could play it properly.

He just practised more and more. But he never even considered himself having a great voice, like Sam Cooke or Johnny Nash or someone. DICKIE JOBSON

Beautiful, beautiful pictures; bring back memories by the score. Everybody firing in their prime... Yeah, primetime. It's wonderful. She did a good job. The public needs to see these pictures, I know that. ASTON 'FAMILY MAN' BARRETT

Before the shows they would smoke all this herb and I didn't know how they could. It seemed to energise everybody as opposed to making them tired. KATE SIMON

You see how calm he is. The calm before the storm. He's just 'Yeaaah...' you know? STEVE JORDAN

Why people drink is they want feeling I get when I smoke herb. Everybody need to get high but some people getting high with the wrong things. When you smoke herb it reveals you to yourself. All the wickedness you do is revealed by the herb – it's your conscience and gives you an honest picture of yourself. BOB MARLEY, 1976

His music is timeless. I get the same feeling when I hear it now as when I heard it the first time. The urgency, the excitement and the gift that every musician would love to have, which is being able to touch people every time they hear your songs.

It's just amazing that Kate was actually able to take pictures like this because it's very easy to just want to put down the camera and watch. It takes a lot of willpower to be able to take these pictures. STEVE JORDAN

When he played live, he was totally absorbed in the music. It wasn't just a ganja-induced trance. He really lived it. You could see it in the way he danced. He was electric when he played live. SPENCER DAVIS

He was like a conductor or a shaman in a trance. The response of the people in Jamaica was the same as the people in Birmingham. Every show I saw was total magic. He put everything into it because for him it was a message. He's not performing. He's not up there like Mick Jagger, jumping around and singing 'Jumpin' Jack Flash'. It was a whole spiritual thing and he was like a preacher preaching his message to the congregation. WAYNE JOBSON

At first he didn't move a lot, but the concerts really changed when he came back from touring England and America. Nobody in Jamaica had ever really seen them as The Wailers; they were still known as Bob Marley and The Wailers. Nobody had really seen them as a group playing 'cos they'd never been a group playing before. They were booked to open for Marvin Gaye at the Carib Theatre, and they blew Marvin Gaye away. The next night they were opening for Marvin Gaye again at the stadium and this time, Marvin Gaye's people put a dead battery in the PA system when he went on. The songs started breaking up and they had to come off stage. But because the songs weren't really working he started moving, and that was one of the first times I'd really seen him doing that.

At that time he didn't have those long locks though. When I first started working with him, he didn't have locks like this. DICKIE JOBSON

Family Man play some nice t'ing for me in the past; and the Bob Marley stuff, that was a Family Man t'ing. Right away. No doubt about it. Like 'Kaya' and 'Soul Revolution' all Family Man, all these songs. LEE 'SCRATCH' PERRY

When I heard Family Man Barrett and Carlton Barrett play together, that was when I was converted. I think that's the way people must have felt the first time they heard Charlie Parker play. I revere them so much.

Family Man Barrett's bass is Jamaica. That's just how it felt. The bass was in the air. It's like being in New Mexico where impressionist paintings are in the clouds. In Jamaica the bass is in the air.

He is the greatest musician I ever photographed. I've photographed a lot of musicians, including Miles Davis, but Fams is the bass man, you know, the base of everything. He took care of me and I'd talk to him a lot. He was always drawing pictures. That's how he'd calm down, doing all these pencil drawings all the time – and they were really good. KATE SIMON

The Barrett brothers were the rhythm section of The Upsetters. When they had their falling out [with Lee 'Scratch' Perry], Bob invited them to come with him and join forces. There's a classic quote that Fams always gives you: 'They were the best vocal group on the island, we were the best rhythm section, so we just decided to come together and mash down the world.' And they did.

ROGER STEFFENS

Barrett brothers are killer man. Anyone will tell you that... Family Man and Carly are the greatest combo ever to play. Family Man heavy, you can't take it from him. From long time, like when I was young – lickle lickle – was always him used to play the bass. When I would sing and I was 14, 15 or 16. JUNIOR DELGADO

 CARLTON BARRETT

When the Barretts came into it, the rhythm became deeper; the music burst into something new.

With all the great things that have been done, that band, that rhythm section, I don't think there's anything better than that. The way that they played, the kaleidoscope of ideas and sounds that Carlton played with Family was a whirlwind. The groove was so intense, and he's playing all this stuff inside it, whipping around like Tasmanian devils, whirling like 'dugga dugga dah dah dugga...' Swirling. And then Aston elongating it, stretching it so that Carly's on top, Aston's filling out the quarter-note values, to where they're behind the beat, and it's just this massive spread, this pillow, this wave. When I played with Aston a few years ago, it was like a dream. I had this gigantic monitor behind me and all I asked for was the bass. So all night I got to play with this bass going, and I've never felt anything like it. I've played with all the great bass players – Willie Weeks, Anthony Jackson, Bob Babbitt, Bob Cranshaw, just to name a few. But Family... it's a whole other thing. STEVE JORDAN

I think that they allowed him a great amount of freedom and creativity. Family Man was a great musician and he had great taste. So it was probably easier working with them than it was with Bunny and Peter, who were very creative but, you know, too many cooks! DICKIE JOBSON

Family Man

Proof. They show me and Bob, my partner and my brother; that's where we make things happen from 1974 straight up onto the past with Bob. Tuning up his guitar. And I set the tone. Yes, the producer, the arranger, the bandleader.
ASTON 'FAMILY MAN' BARRETT

We were always double checking. Family Man would check everybody's sound; Bob would check the sound and I would check my sound. You see Tyrone playing bass; we played bits of each other's instruments so we knew what each other was doing. JUNIOR MARVIN

Every person played every other instrument in the band, so they knew how each song fit together, and why Bob wanted it the way he wanted it. And then in performance, if the spirit moved him, 'Get Up, Stand Up' could be four minutes on Monday night, 17 minutes on Tuesday, then 12 minutes, and two nights later 21 minutes. He would just kind of flick a finger, or raise an eyebrow, and the band would shift where he wanted to take them. He'd make up verses you'd never heard before. It's astonishing, and that's why I have probably 3,000 hours of Marley tapes: because he never did the same show twice, the songs were always varied. And the band never knew: 'Oh gosh, is he going to string out "Them Belly Full" tonight, or are we going to do a 14 minute "Exodus"? Or what's he going to turn this song into a medley of? We've gotta be prepared.'
ROGER STEFFENS

He was a perfectionist. He wouldn't really ever be pleased; don't care how much the crowd were tearing the place down, Bob wouldn't return for encores if he didn't think the band played so good! But when the band played really good, he soared. He would put new lyrics in and he'd go to another level.

He put everything into the music. He was very serious about his mission. He wasn't just a pop star, it was about a message of one love, that everyone should get together and talk.

He saw himself more as a messenger, someone who was put here to try and pull everyone together. NEVILLE GARRICK

We played some weird places. I remember Tivoli Gardens [in Copenhagen] – a fairground where they had summer festivals every year. It's a big place and a nice venue. JUNIOR MARVIN

Just look at that, they're working it out, you know? I love this picture... You know, they're going to play, and they're gonna kick it! That's amazing! STEVE JORDAN

It was almost a spiritual experience. I was blessed to see so many performances. Bob didn't actually perform very often in Jamaica himself, but when he did it was very special. But so many times I've had the privilege of concentrating on different aspects of the performances and it was like a religious experience. He was connecting with your head; he was freeing your spirit; he was teaching you something, not just entertaining. They often say an artist needs to look at the audience to connect: Bob really didn't. His eyes were closed, he was in deep meditation, sometimes almost in a trance. DERA TOMPKINS

I said to Bob once, 'I'm trying to get a picture of you with your eyes open and it's hard!' So after that in the song 'Exodus', when he would sing, 'Open your eyes and look within!' he would open his eyes wide on the word 'open'. I would get one opportunity per night. KATE SIMON

What made Bob such a star was his charisma. He was so charismatic. You look at him and know he's going somewhere no one else is. SPENCER DAVIS

I have a duty to tell the truth as I have been told it. I will keep on doing it until I am satisfied the people have the message that Rastafari is the Almighty and all we black people have redemption just like anyone else. Not for money will I do anything, but because I have something to do. BOB MARLEY, 1976

I am neither on the right side nor on the left side, I go straight ahead. Nobody thinks about going straight ahead. Do you understand? Do you remember when they crucified the Christ? There was someone on the left and someone on the right. They were both thieves! It's the same for ideologies. BOB MARLEY, 1980

Common sense is the best technology, seen? Going to space and all of that, I don't think it really worth it. And plenty other things too. Even the atom, this-and-that. Technology can be mis-philosophy. BOB MARLEY, 1979

TUFF GONG
UPRISING EUROPE 80

The I-Three were always a very special part of Bob's concerts. The way they moved together, the way they really related to Bob and of course the voices. They had a great blend. RANDALL GRASS

I loved Judy, Rita and Marcia; they were really elegant, sophisticated, intelligent women.

I remember how odd it was that you'd be hearing them going, 'Total destruction/The only solution.' These three little birds singing this stuff. KATE SIMON

When The I-Three joined, the music just began growing and evolving: they were able to engage in the caller-response, African way of singing. That's just an amazing musical element only enhanced by the rhythm section. STEVE JORDAN

Marcia, of course, is just a great singer. If Jamaica has a first lady of songs she's it. Because she's had hits in virtually every era since the mid-Sixties in Jamaica. She's underappreciated. RANDALL GRASS

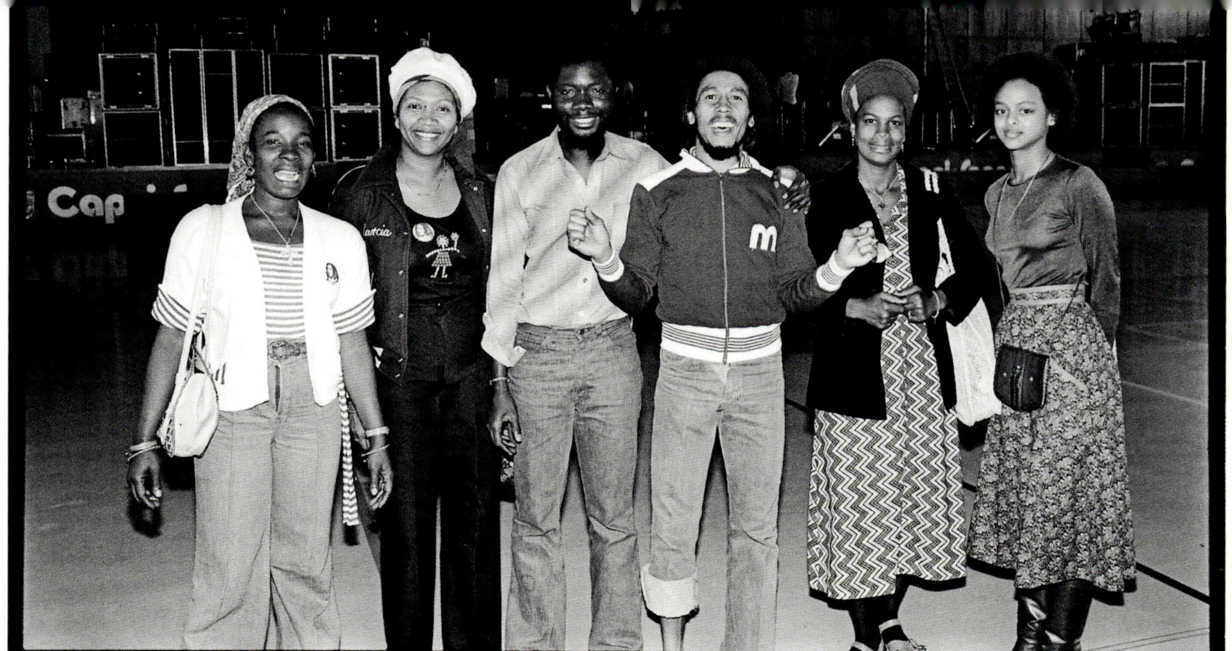

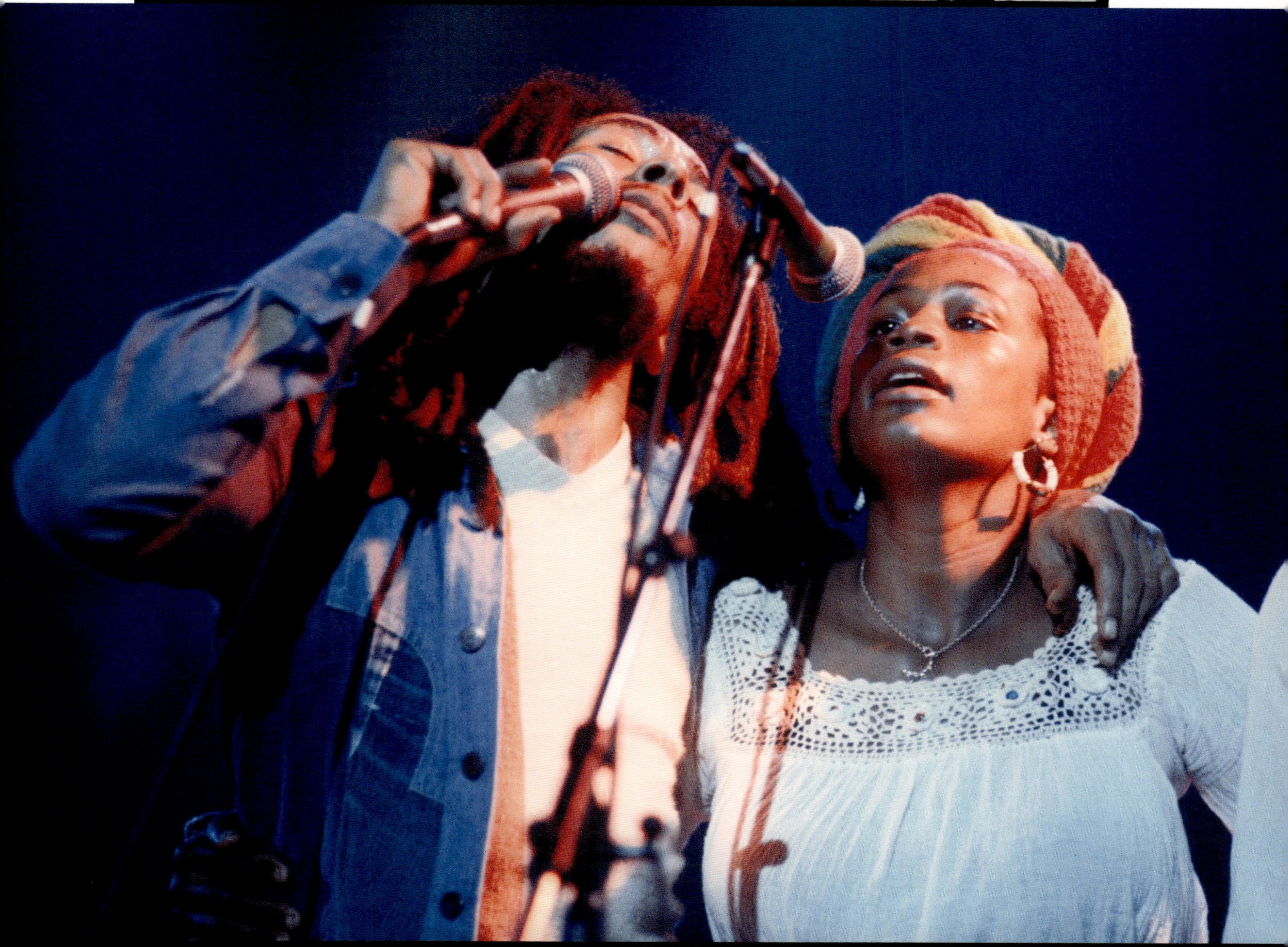

BOB MARLEY & THE WAILERS
Exodus

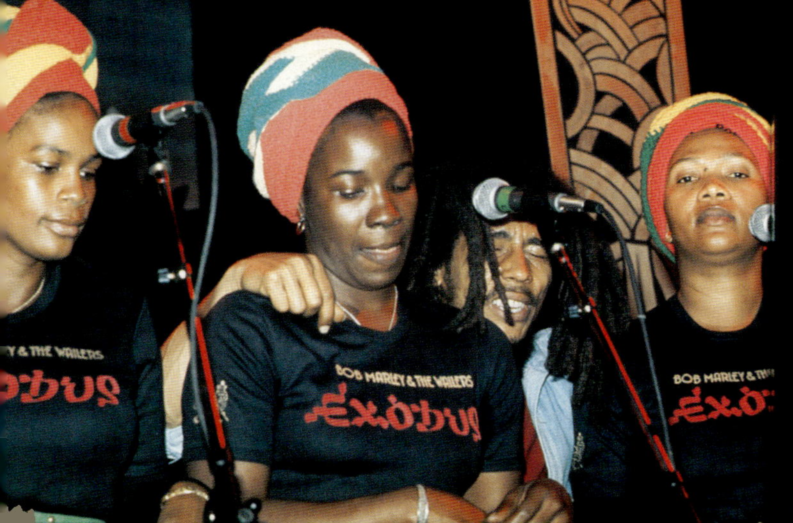

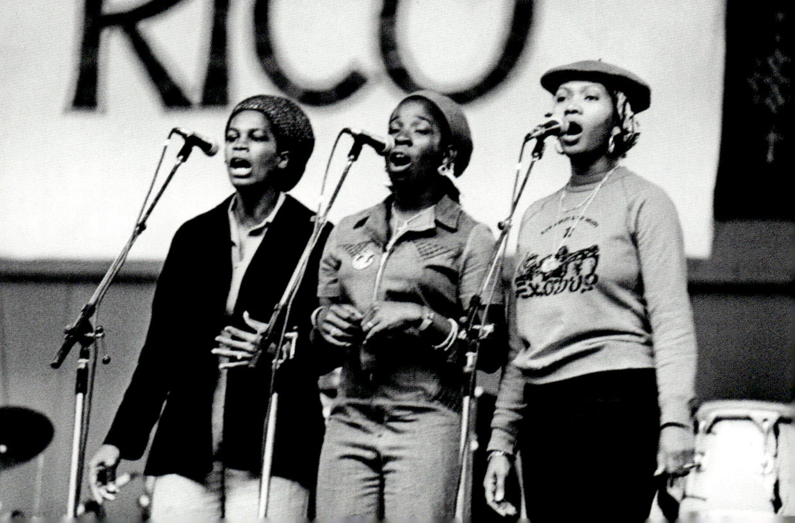

RICO

What a scary picture. That's a scary picture that... Raasclaat! DAVID KENNEDY

They are unprecedented pictures! They're blood curdling. Because we know now that that's the period of time when they were trying to get him to amputate his foot. ROGER STEFFENS

I was taking pictures of them playing football in this huge hangar – I think the words 'Real is Real' were in the back in German – and over at the side there were are all these artificial limbs and braces you would need if your bones and chest are weak. The pictures tell the whole story: I took three frames and his expression seems to develop. It's like he's stopped in this reverie.

The pictures suggest to me he was thinking one thing, which is: 'Raasclaat!' I don't think a woman can say that but... please fill in an appropriate American equivalent. KATE SIMON

In the years working with Bob, I watched him grow and saw the discipline, the commitment, training and dedication. 'Cos he was a soccer fanatic, and I was playing premier league soccer in Jamaica, so he always loved to train with us. And we trained hard. We worked hard, and he was right there with us, 'cos he was a fanatic. He just loved soccer, and music. That's his thing. It was all part of the greatness. Taking care of himself, good food, exercising a lot. ANTONIO 'GILLIE' GILBERT

Bob loved his football, and nothing was going to stop him. Not even a bandaged toe.
KATE SIMON

Football was really his second love. He was good. I don't think he would have made a pro team but he was good. Because of his height he was a very aggressive type of player. He always wanted to be 'Skill' Cole, ya know? NEVILLE GARRICK

How Bob could play all that football and go on stage and play like he did, with all the ganja he smoked... it's beyond me. SPENCER DAVIS

Bob always like me as a soccer player. My mannerism, the way I play soccer, I'm always serious, no nonsense, know what I'm saying? And he's a soccer player, he loves soccer. He and Bunny they loved soccer... Peter wasn't that much in tune to it. He was more into that karate, kung fu thing, yoga or whatever. But Bob and Bunny loved playing soccer, loved competitive games. They were pretty good.

When we were on tour, the promoter always had a team within each city or country play us a game. We played in London, France, Belgium, Australia, you name it. Most of the time we won. Because he had some good players with him! I was a top player at the time. ANTONIO 'GILLIE' GILBERT

We played everywhere. Before the show, he'd warm up in the dressing room keeping up headers with Gillie, and the ball wouldn't touch the ground. For maybe half an hour, the ball wouldn't touch the ground. Bob wanted to play for Manchester United, or Liverpool or something like that. Even though he had bandages on he still wanted to play. I suppose it was quite good on tour because it kept him fit, but…

Seeco was a good player, Neville was an OK player, Gillie was a very good player. One of Bob's former managers was Allan 'Skill' Cole, who was Jamaica's best soccer player ever. He played for a Brazilian team, the first Jamaican to do so, and they actually came to Jamaica to beg for him, so he was good! JUNIOR MARVIN

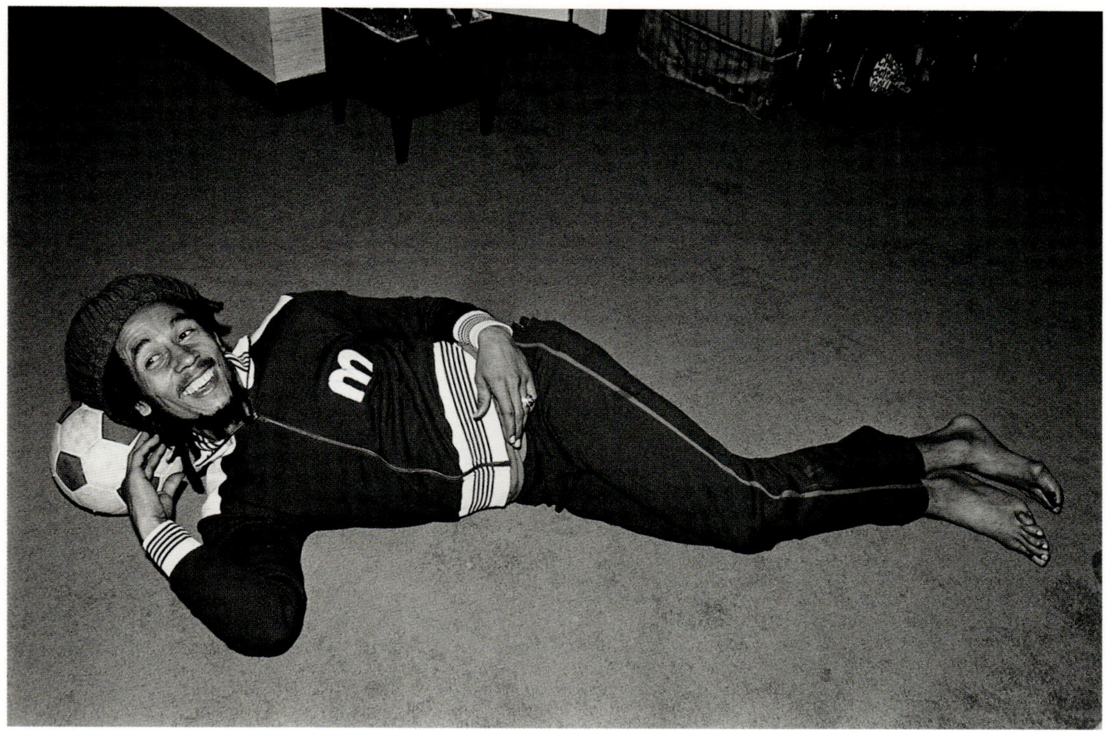

Bob and I, Junior Marvin and Jacob Miller, we all went in a private plane to Brazil for the opening of BMG's office there.

And he loved it in Brazil. He was totally mobbed and on the way back he was kind of picking 'Could You Be Loved' out on the guitar for the first time. CHRIS BLACKWELL

We went to Brazil and we played soccer with some of the world's best players. Jim Capaldi, the drummer from Traffic, was there and we made up a team and won this tournament. It was Bob's dream to play soccer in Brazil. Jacob Miller said to me, 'Imagine, I come all the way to Brazil and look who I end up playing with!' Because I wasn't really considered the greatest player. I played pretty well in the games that we played; I scored the first goal which kinda redeemed me, and then we won the tournament so my first goal got things going! JUNIOR MARVIN

Bob Marley play sweet football. Gillie's good. He tall, Gillie-dread; Gillie-dread a baller but Bob Marley a wicked baller too. Gillie-dread ah stand up on the ball and show it so ya c'yan take it away! He's a good player but him stand up on it and say, 'Move it!'

Gillie used to play in a team called House of Dread. Me was a baller too. Me used to play for a team called Trafford, after Old Trafford [the home of Manchester United]. JUNIOR DELGADO

She [Kate] was kind of a little rough and tight; uptight. Because, you know, to get everybody together is a hell of a job. So it take me awhile then I really notice, I say, 'She needs to get a group shot.' And I never stop pushing the vibes until I get close that she could get something done.

We were doing our thing, you know? She was taking pictures when she can but she was not much pleased because she wanted a full, direct picture with Bob and the band and everybody moving so fast from rehearsal to soundcheck to show, doing the move thing. Then one time she get real sad and I say, 'No, I'm gonna help you out at this, I'm gonna situate this band; you gotta get a good picture of the band, you gotta have something to take back. ASTON 'FAMILY MAN' BARRETT

This gig was great. There were more people outside, I believe, than actually inside. It was electric. It was very similar to what he did at the Lyceum a couple of years before, but there were even more people this time. It was quite a small venue and I think we did four shows there. We recorded all of them, and made what's probably one of the best live videos ever.

I actually grew up around two miles from here in North London. JUNIOR MARVIN

I'll tell you something, at the end of this Exodus tour, I got back to America after doing the Rainbow and I couldn't talk for five days. KATE SIMON

ONE LOVE

Bob's self-imposed exile from Jamaica lasted 14 months from the end of December 1976 to early 1978. During this time, Jamaica had become increasingly violent. To add to the already lethal mix of drugs, guns and whispers of CIA influence, the warring political parties had continued a policy of divide and rule, recruiting street-tough rude boys to their so-called causes.

As street violence escalated, two ranking gunmen from either side of the political divide found themselves sharing a prison cell. Against all the odds, instead of beating each other to death, they realised that they were being used as political pawns and decided to call a truce.

To mark it, they wanted to hold a concert on 22 April, 1978, the 12th anniversary of Haile Selassie I's visit to Jamaica, with Bob Marley as the headline act.

Obviously, Bob wasn't too keen to return from exile to such a violent, politically heated climate. Even less so to play live; the last time he had done so in Jamaica it had nearly cost him his life.

However, the Twelve Tribes Rastafarian leaders were backing the event, and representatives of both rival gangs travelled to London to guarantee Bob his safety.

The rest is history. The One Love Peace Concert went ahead with some of the greatest names in reggae, including Dillinger, Big Youth, Jacob Miller and Culture.

Peter Tosh had been reluctant to play – he was suspicious of anything associated with 'politrickery' – but his set was captivating. He spent much of it openly taunting and haranguing the assembled political leaders as thunder and lightning rolled in from the hills behind, adding their damnation to his. His main criticism was of the government's oppressive stance towards users of herb, so he lit up a king-cone-sized spliff right in front of them. Some weeks later, he was arrested and beaten close to death.

The album *Kaya* had been released just months before the concert. Perhaps the most mellow album of Bob's career – full of love songs and paeans to marijuana, 'kaya' being a Jamaican term for herb – Bob's performance was still no less political than Peter's. Stating: 'I'm not so good at talking...' he went on to make one of the most visually powerful statements any artist has ever made. The bringing together of the country's warring political leaders in front of a crowd of 40,000 people was so momentous it would be a significant factor in the United Nations' decision to award him the peace medal 'on behalf of 500 million Africans'.

Hanging out at Hope Road was always great. It was a great place to relax for any number of reasons. Someone was always out back playing music. They were putting a studio in and there was a lot of rehearsal going on. There were always people knocking a soccer ball around the back yard and Bob had a ping pong table set up out on the porch. It was an incredible place to be around. JEFF WALKER

Bob's house had a huge garden in the back and there was a studio and a kind of record store where Family Man helped me pick out a bunch of singles to take back to New York. It kind of reminded me of a Key West house. It had a really interesting doorway with an illustration of the Twelve Tribes on it. The last place I shot Bob was in front of that door. KATE SIMON

When Bob moved there he would be the one doing the gardening. He wouldn't just hire a gardener, he'd be digging and fixing things up and working along with everybody. It wasn't him shouting from somewhere, 'Plant this!' or 'Do that!' or 'That doesn't look good!' He never shouted out orders. I guess people who are natural leaders are like that; people just keep an eye on them and want to make them smile. CHRIS BLACKWELL

During my time growing up it was a much gentler Jamaica. I think it got violent when things started happening like elections. Guns started coming onto the island, and political gangs started to be formed.

For example, Trench Town was a slum. The trench was really a gully carrying fluids from the city to the sea. Every big city brings people from the rural areas looking for better, so they end up living in shanty towns. So, we had a lot of places like we used to call Back-A-Wall, which is now Tivoli Gardens – which I found out while touring with Bob is also the name of an amusement park in Europe! When the JLP [the right wing Jamaican Labour Party] got into power, they knocked down Back-A-Wall, knocked down the shanties, knocked down the market where people would come from the country and sell their produce, and they built a housing project. Then those people who got those houses became loyal to the JLP. Whenever they have an election they get 150 per cent of the vote! And then when the PNP [People's National Party] got in power, they built Trench Town, which is to the west of Tivoli Gardens, and those people became ardent supporters of the PNP. These people, during their ruling party's time, they don't have to pay their electricity bills and stuff. These people are fed up so they will do anything to keep their party in power. That is when the violence came into the housing projects. NEVILLE GARRICK

When Bob first moved to Trench Town there was a lot of crime; it was poor but there was a lot of creative people... DICKIE JOBSON

Kingston is a city. It has its toughness and its beauty. It was almost like heaven and hell because there was so much struggle in the streets – constant in the ghettos because of the political fighting – but there was just as much love and community and exchange between people. I was there when the elections came up and many people died. There was almost war in the ghettos. But I was also there for the period when there was the One Love concert, when there was the truce and Jamaica came together. There is a wisdom that comes from being poor and having to struggle and that energy is a resourcefulness that is very evident in Kingston. As tough as things were, there was a life, there was an energy. I compare it to the Harlem Renaissance. I think years later we are going to look back and see it like that. I've never been in a community where all of my friends and my comrades were artists. Everyone could sing, everyone could play an instrument; there was a studio session every night and there was a show on the weekends. Everyone would get dressed up in their colours and it was exciting. It was a beehive of activity and energy. There was good food, there was music, there was soccer, there was reasoning with people who didn't sit and watch TV. People sat down and we talked about African history; we talked about the politics in America; we talked about the black struggle; we talked about the Black Panthers. People loved to engage in conversation which is probably an art which we've lost. Reasoning was at the foundation of the social exchange in the community. DERA TOMPKINS

Jamaica's a paradise for some and a pair of dice for others... DON LETTS

They say that it's this male dominated culture, but I felt that the women were really running the show down there. On the tour bus, for instance, the women sat at the front. They were really well respected and treated. I was never hassled at all in Jamaica, not once.

Before I got to Jamaica, I was schooled in phrases I needed to know in order to navigate Kingston; 'irie', 'I and I' and 'ital'. The more time I spent there, the more phrases I learned, like 'overstand', which I always liked: to understand something really deeply. Expressions like 'serious t'ing', 'politricks', 'na true?' and 'soon come' – it's not just the word, but how you work the word. And it's not such a big step from that to the creation of the music. KATE SIMON

Word sound is power. They had that much respect for the word! ROGER STEFFENS

One time, we had gunmen in our hotel room; I think they'd called a truce for about 13 minutes or something. Politically I could never follow all this stuff. But I felt that I was in, for want of a better word, a pretty 'heavy' place. KATE SIMON

It got heavier in the '70s. Oh my God, the weed and the crack cocaine... Jamaica became an international player in narcotics. At one time in those early days, Jamaica was the number one supplier of herb. Bigger than anybody in the world. They planted and shipped billions and billions of pounds of marijuana. I mean, Morgan The Pirate lived in Jamaica; Jamaica's a pirate country. DANNY SIMS

You can tell, just by looking at these pictures, that all these disparate people were comfortable in front of Kate's camera. Another person might have gone in there and been antagonistic or abrasive such that these people would not have allowed themselves to be photographed. ROGER STEFFENS

There were a lot of political problems; there was a dip in tourism and there were riots going on. We certainly felt insulated from it. I drove all over the island without ever encountering anything. I mean, I've got stories of encounters with the police and the army and all of that, but the atmosphere... it was magical. It was one of the most incredible experiences I've ever had. The night of Bob's attempted assassination and the following Smile Jamaica concert was as close to a combat situation or atmosphere that I ever care to be in. But it doesn't really take away from the experience. JEFF WALKER

Where Bob's yard was in Trench Town, they've fixed it up now. Not long ago, I was down there with some serious, very righteous Rasta guys, and they said that some people from the JLP were trying to take over the area. They wanted to have it because they realised that all the tourists want to go there. All those areas around Trench Town, places like Jonestown and Denham Town, they're pure murder. The rest of Jamaica is not like this – Jamaica's a safe place – it's only this two square miles in downtown Kingston which are pure murder and Trench Town's right in the middle of it. But they have to keep this little area safe to bring the spring-breakers in. They need the money from it, because people down there have nothing to eat.

So the Rasta guy I know there is telling me that the JLP were trying to buy up houses so they could control the yard; but the guys living in the yard, and all the Rastas round there say, 'We're not giving up this place, because it's like Bob has told us to keep it, and this is our only source of income.'

So at the same time as he's being very spiritual, this Rasta said that when the JLP sent their gunmen over to come and take the place, 'I just went up into the roof and got out my machine gun.' So, it's all peace and love but if you come through that gate... But down there you don't have a machine gun because you want to, but because you need it for protection. When these fuckers come you better be able to keep them out, or they'll just come and kill all of you, take away the area, and all of a sudden somebody else is living in your house. So they have the gun there to protect the yard while the tourists come and buy T-shirts or whatever.
WAYNE JOBSON

B
Snack Counter
BOX MILK
ORANGE JUICE
SANDWICH
BOIL EGGS
ETC

"BEHOLD"
THE
LACKHEART
MAN
ble at all leading Re ord Shops
BLACKHEART MAN
NOW AVAILABLE
at all leading Record Sho
PEARL & DEAN OUTDOOR ADVERTISING
'S SNAC COU
FOR SOFT DR
COLD BEER SKY JUIC

After the Exodus tour, the next time I saw Bob was at the rehearsal for the One Love Peace Concert at the National Stadium. He seemed really serious to me. I guess, because of the political import of the circumstances, he had reason to be. His brow was furrowed, he was solemn and I can only imagine it was because of the gravity of the situation. His frame of mind was totally different. I remember, I went on stage during the soundcheck. Bob was preoccupied. KATE SIMON

The problem is the law that govern the country. What kind of spiritual well being, what kind of struggle ya go through? Put care of the whole place to the Rasta, then the government care for the people and so there would be no suffering; everything would'na come on. But the people can't get a chance to be themselves, so everyone suffer for that. BOB MARLEY, 1979

One time Bob was on tour in San Diego, I was with the Stones in LA and Mick decided he wanted to jam with Bob. A plane was duly chartered, a limousine hired, and I was sent to pick him up. When I got there, I told him the Stones wanted to jam with him. He took one look at the limo and got on the tour bus. That sort of summed him up, you know? Like, who needs The Rolling Stones? I called Mick and told him what happened and said, 'I guess he doesn't want to jam with you,' and he said, 'Don't worry man, we've got Pete Tosh.' Which sort of summed him up too. SPENCER DAVIS

This is Mick Jagger and Chris Blackwell at the One Love Peace Concert. Mick Jagger had no money on him and so he and Earl McGrath were hitting on me for cash. Ironic. He still owes me five dollars. KATE SIMON

I don't remember Mick being there, but I was certainly at that concert. We were probably all there together and just touched base at different times but I don't remember it. I remember being completely enthralled by the concert and Bob's performance. It was like he was taken over by a higher power or something. He was barely touching the ground. CHRIS BLACKWELL

Bob had been in exile from the shooting and the people who were responsible for those activities were never caught.

I still don't know who did it. I know some of the people who came, but why? Whether it was political or whether it was simply about a bad debt from the Jamaican mafia for a horse race scam, or maybe some combination of the two, I don't know what to believe any more. It wasn't really a professional hit at all; a professional hit man would have stayed there until they were all dead on the floor and then left instead of just spraying indiscriminately, wounding people and killing nobody. Anyhow, two of the chief gunmen from the rival political parties, Bucky Marshall and Claude Massop, are locked up in prison some time after the assassination attempt and Manley's re-election, and put in the same prison cell. Maybe Manley thought they'd just beat each other to death, I don't know, but instead they started comparing notes and declared a truce between themselves. Word got out and that's how the peace truce started.

Eventually they were released, flew to England and said to Bob: 'Look, there's a spontaneous peace truce that has sprung up in western Kingston, in the ghettos, and we want to celebrate this truce on the 12th anniversary of Haile Selassie's visit to Jamaica, on 22 April, 1978, under a full moon. And we want you to headline the concert.'

Bob was very apprehensive. They'd tried to kill him once, what's he going back to? He'd been an exile for 14 months but they ultimately succeeded in convincing him that it would be safe for him to return. He does so at the end of February.

On the night he stands up in front of 40,000 people at the end of an eight-hour concert, and finishing his set he makes the prime minister and the leader of the opposition come on stage and shake hands as he stands between them.

Bob was jumping up and down singing, 'I'm waiting, I'm waiting', and there's no Manley. Finally he gives up and he turns round to Seaga to bring him up to the mic and Manley comes across the stage. Bob was beside himself, leaping over the mic. ROGER STEFFENS

We don't like politicians.
Peter Tosh used to call it 'politricks'. ANTONIO 'GILLIE' GILBERT

Bob came out and put Seaga and Manley together. I looked around and realised that the front of the stage, which had been crowded, was suddenly deserted. It was eerie. Perhaps because I was working I didn't take time to think I might have been in jeopardy; that people left because they thought something was going to go down. KATE SIMON

If you look at the footage of that concert, he was definitely connected that night. He was definitely on a mission. Serious. DERA TOMPKINS

He was amazed, you know? The youth took it on themselves to create this peace initiative and he left the island because of that same political violence and his attempted assassination. They figured that if he came back it would symbolise the peace. The concert was planned to commemorate the visit of Haile Selassie to Jamaica in 1966. It was tremendous. Peter Tosh lambasted the government and then Bob had to upstage that by bringing the two political rival leaders together.

I think that concert and the Zimbabwe independence concert are two of the most important shows Bob has ever done, politically. NEVILLE GARRICK

Bob Marley shake it up bad man but Peter did go on wicked! The audience love it! After that, them did have a plan and they beat up Peter fe the speech he make. JUNIOR DELGADO

Who could have done that other than Bob? To take both sides and bring them together? Because Bob was not with either side. Bob was neutral. He was bigger than those guys as a popular figure. Bob Marley was the Minister of Goodwill for Jamaica. When you go out and draw the kind of people he drew, sell the kind of records he sold around the world, Jamaica was put on the map. It wasn't just ganja that put Jamaica on the map; it was Bob Marley and ganja. DANNY SIMS

Neville Garrick once said that moment was like Christ on the cross between the two thieves. We showed Bob a video of that concert in LA, in 1979, the first time he had ever seen it. Afterwards John Sutton-Smith – a friend of mine who worked on the film *Heartland Reggae* – asked him what was going through his mind when he stood between those two guys, in whose names so many thousands of people had been murdered. Bob said 'Well, I man no politician, but if I man a politician, only one thing for me to do at that moment. Kill them both.' And then he disappeared into a bedroom. That was the last I ever saw of Bob. ROGER STEFFENS

I would have loved to have been there. It would have taken me full circle [from seeing the Smile Jamaica concert, the day of the assassination attempt on Bob].

Coming out of the Sixties in the States, with the association between music and the anti-war and the civil rights movement, the political nature of Bob's music didn't seem odd to me. But I was always aware that Bob was such an important artist that it had become a mission to do what we could to get his message out. But that message was never political. I think he was very clear – even with the Smile Jamaica concert – that this was not intended as a political endorsement for anyone but essentially as an endorsement for peace. JEFF WALKER

It's like any kind of peace process. We have it in the Middle East; we have it in some places in Africa; we have it right here in the United States in some ways. It's an ongoing process, and we have to keep pedalling. If we stop pedalling the bicycle stops and the process stops. You have to keep working, even when it looks like there's just one too many suicide bombers, or one too many assassinations, one too many mysterious disappearances, or just out-and-out gruesome acts of violence. We have to keep working for peace. We cannot stop working for peace. And that's what Bob's message was. No matter what, you cannot stop working for peace. That's the most important thing. STEVE JORDAN

I asked Peter Tosh if there was any difference since the peace treaty was signed and he said, 'Yeah. More dead.' ROGER STEFFENS

A year before him dead, me and him sit up on that step; me, him and Dennis Brown.
A year before him dead, and he give me a long stalk of sensimilla... JUNIOR DELGADO

THANKS AND PRAISES

On 24 April, 1978, two days after the One Love Peace Concert, I went to 56 Hope Road and shot these pictures. I never took Bob Marley's photograph again. KATE SIMON

In 1979 Bob Marley became the first reggae act to headline New York's legendary Apollo Theatre in Harlem. In 1980, while other musicians might have been opening supermarkets, Bob Marley opened a whole new nation playing at Zimbabwe's independence day celebrations. He was greeted as one of their own and showed his legendary generosity in paying for the stage, crew and equipment to be shipped over from the US himself. He played two nights. On the first, supposedly reserved for dignitaries including HRH Prince Charles, Prince of Wales – there to represent the retreating British Empire – freedom fighters stuck outside the gates forced their way in and the band were interrupted by tear gas and a near riot. The second night they played a free gig for the Zimbabwean people, without the presence of officials. Leaving the stage after their set, fully expecting to play many more hours in encores, the band were surprised to see the crowds wandering off. They hadn't realised that the people of Zimbabwe had never attended a live concert before and had no concept of encores or crowd etiquette.

Bob's career was on a high, but his health, sadly, wasn't. The cancer detected in his toe back in 1977 hadn't gone away. He had been to see various doctors and most had recommended amputation. Losing his big toe would almost certainly have meant an end to his beloved football, and his shamanic on-stage dancing.

In September of 1980, in the middle of a run of dates at New York's Madison Square Garden, Bob collapsed while out jogging in Central Park. The cancer had spread throughout his body. In desperation, he flew to Germany for experimental treatment with the controversial Dr Issels. It was all in vain. Weak, skinny and dread-less, he returned to his mother's house in Miami. Just days later, on 11 May 1981, he died at the Cedars of Lebanon Hospital. His body flown back to Jamaica, the same government that had persecuted Rastafarians, herb users and sufferahs like Bob for so long afforded him a state funeral.

> **'His message was a protest against injustice, a comfort for the oppressed. He stood there, performed there, his message reached there and everywhere. Today's funeral service is an international right of a native son. He was born in a humble cottage nine miles from Alexandria in the parish of St Ann. He lived in the western section of Kingston as a boy where he joined in the struggle of the ghetto. He learned the message of survival in his boyhood days in Kingston's west end. But it was his raw talent, unswerving discipline and sheer perseverance that transported him from just another victim of the ghetto to the top ranking superstar in the entertainment industry of the third world.'** PRIME MINISTER EDWARD SEAGA – speaking at the funeral

OFFICIAL FUNERAL SERVICE OF THE
ATE HON. ROBERT NESTA MARLEY O.M

I'd heard stories that he was ill, but you couldn't believe it and you didn't want to believe it and nobody was really talking about it. I'd hear a rumour that something was wrong with Bob, I'd check it out and somebody would say that no, it wasn't true. Everybody was denying that Bob was perilously ill.

Bob always used to call me Kate Si-mon and the last time I saw him he was walking up 57th Street, right outside my flat now. He was walking out of a health food restaurant; he sees me and he shouts, 'Kate Simon, wha'appen?'

On 21 September, 1980, he had a seizure in Central Park, not far from the last place I'd seen him. KATE SIMON

Cancer was an American disease not a Jamaican disease. It's a food disease. With Jamaicans eating so much fish, they get Omega-6, Omega-9, Omega-3: all the three fatty acids. In America, we're eating grease. We're eating pigs, chickens and cows and we're eating goats and hogs. Jamaicans are living on the sea. You can have a great meal in Jamaica free: all you have to do is go out on the water, put your hand in and take a fish out. DANNY SIMS

I had heard about his foot and then I heard that it had spread to his brain. There were rumours that he was in Ethiopia, that he was here, he was there; nobody was quite sure where he was. Through my connections I had heard that Bob was in Germany. His personal doctor, Pee Wee Fraser, called me. He had gone to Harvard with me and knew that I was a medical librarian. He said, 'Dera, I would like you to do a search on melanoma and black people.' The rest of the day I did a literature search. I read as many articles as I could about melanoma in black people and then I really understood the depth of Bob's condition. This was December. I think he had checked in to the clinic in November and I realised that the end was imminent. Short of a miracle, things did not look good. Bob was not just ill, he was terminally ill.

What I did discover by reading the literature was that melanoma is not a condition that black people contract; it is a European condition. When black people do have this condition it often begins with a mole and it becomes cancerous sometime after puberty. The moles are usually on the bottom of the foot or the palm of the hand, where there's less pigment. So I knew the whole story: I knew that Bob was possibly in stage four at this time, the fourth of a five-year life span. It is fatal. Melanoma is fatal. I understand that when he'd gone to Sloan Kettering Hospital [in New York] they basically told him that they could make him comfortable. Going to Doctor Issels's clinic [in Germany] was a last hope. DERA TOMPKINS

I took him to a doctor on Harley Street, London. That was the doctor who told him to amputate the toe. Of course, everyone said, 'Oh! It's a conspiracy! Junior is a good friend of Chris Blackwell, the contract's almost up, they're trying to make you lose your balance, trying to make you not such a good artist!' Because once you lose your big toe you lose your balance. Losing his toe meant he wouldn't be able to dance his magical dance anymore. A lot of people were saying, 'Bob, you're not gonna be able to dance on stage anymore, you're not gonna be able to play soccer anymore. Blackwell obviously wants you to stay with Island so they're trying to think up ways to hold you back, and Junior's a friend of Blackwell.' I was like: Woah! Hold on a minute! I was just happy to take him to a doctor, that's all.

But in those days there was a million people whispering in his ear, 'Bob do this, Bob do that.' In the end he always made up his own mind, but if you have a lot of people trying to influence you it can just confuse you. I'm pretty sure he would always listen to himself in the final analysis. JUNIOR MARVIN

I never saw him smile again. Never. What I saw was pure devastation. He always carried a perpetual smile on his face; always had that certain kind of shy smile. From the moment he was told, I never saw it again. He was devastated. Absolutely devastated. You could feel it.

He had everything. He'd just sold out Madison Square Garden in about two minutes. Two shows – gone. He could have sold a week out. He was on a roll. He had just played to 110,000 people in Milan, 85,000 people in Turin, and 58,000 people in Paris. In America we put the tickets on sale and the tickets were gone before we could say: 'We're open.' And all of a sudden somebody's telling him that's all gone. That was a miserable, miserable feeling. DANNY SIMS

A major daily newspaper called me to go down to Jamaica and cover Bob's funeral.

When I got down to Kingston, I began photographing the scenes leading up to and including the funeral, with no other direction from the paper that hired me. It was odd to get no communication as to what I was supposed to be getting. Finally, I ran into the paper's representatives at the bar in the hotel and they said to me that I was probably one of the only photographers that could get close enough to get a picture of Bob lying in state. They said there would be money in it for me. I said, 'Consider it done.' Of course, I had no intention of doing it. I didn't want to see Bob lying in state and I didn't want us to remember him that way. I would never have photographed him like that, but I figured that if I was emphatic that it was a done deal, they wouldn't ask the myriad other photographers who were already down there to do it. I'd like to think, therefore, that I had something to do with the fact that there is no photograph of Bob lying in state.

I've never seen a funeral like this, before or since, on film or in real life. It was something Cecil B DeMille couldn't have staged.

It was all of life and death coming on. First there was the Kingston National Arena and the service with the Ethiopian priests, which was quite some spectacle. There was Rita [Marley] and [Michael] Manley and [Prime Minister Edward] Seaga, Bob's children, and all the other luminaries who showed up, like Roberta Flack. There were all these soldiers in uniform, the pageantry and the priests. I remember standing by the casket and my legs started to give way. I was right next to it.

After that I got in a truck to join the funeral cortege. Bob was in another blue flatbed truck which broke down on the way to St Ann. I was sitting next to Adrian Boot and the two of us drove all the way, right behind, shooting the entire island. And the island came out like it was New Orleans. I mean, the island wasn't sad; people were booming Bob Marley music all the way from Kingston to St Ann, the streets lined several rows deep with people.

It was wonderful. They were telling him they loved him. Everybody has to die; dying is a part of life. Of course, Bob was so young, but I liked that they were celebrating his life like that. Anyway, we got to St Ann and it was like something out of *The Ten Commandments*: the whole mountainside was covered with people. **KATE SIMON**

"THE WICKED IS DRIVEN AWAY IN HIS WICKEDNESS: BUT THE RIGHTEOUS HATH HOPE IN HIS DEATH."
PROVERBS.c.14:vs.32.
HON. ROBERT NESTA MARLEY O.M.
BOB MARLEY AND THE WAILERS

I wasn't surprised at the way the authorities tried to hijack the funeral. Politics is politics, you know? They use every moment to their advantage and this was a big chance for them. The whole world was there; they had international press, dignitaries from all over, artists who had come to pay their respects, people in the business who came to pay their respects. It's pretty much who you know not what you know, and politicians, they want to be known.

There was a concert at the funeral, on stage at the National Arena. Cedella Booker – Bob's mother – and Ziggy and Steven [Bob's sons] and The I-Three were all there; that was a kind of farewell, you know? All the band were there, except maybe for Tyrone, I think, who was pretty much emotionally overcome by then. JUNIOR MARVIN

I went down to the National Arena to see his body in state. What a tragedy for the country. Everyone felt that they lost their own son, their brother, their father. But because of the songs and the mission and the message, yes, it became like a celebration: a jubilee going to Nine Mile.

But what an experience to travel across the belly of Jamaica like that, to the north coast to see where Bob was born in this country area. After that you had a different understanding of where Bob's imagery came from. It completed the cycle. His story is just so full of significant moments, from Smile Jamaica to the One Love concert to the Zimbabwe independence celebrations. He made a great contribution to the world.

When Bob was gone, I knew there was a gap there that no one could fill. It was more than six years before The Wailers really did anything again. He was their leader; respected and rightfully so. They moved together, joked together, hung together, ate and celebrated together; they were a unit. But without the cornerstone, well... Bob's place has never been taken yet. DERA TOMPKINS

The day of his funeral was a really sad day. The turnout of people was incredible. All the way around Kingston from the ceremony and then all the way to Nine Mile, the street was full all the way. And the hillside was covered with people. CHRIS BLACKWELL

That's quite a sheer mountainside. I was there recently; it felt like it was almost straight up and down and the pictures show it covered with people. It's amazing nobody was killed! If one person had fallen it could have started an avalanche.
ROGER STEFFENS

It must have been the night after the funeral, myself and Fred Schruers – who was there for *The Washington Post* – went over to Tuff Gong Studios. I saw Marcia Griffiths there and I seem to remember Jimmy Cliff there too. I certainly remember Fred calling in his story for the *Post*.

Bob's mother sang; how brilliantly his mother sang. It was gut-wrenchingly beautiful.

I hadn't looked at these pictures for about 20 years and when I did, it broke my heart. I think that while I was at the funeral, I was using the camera as a veil so that when I was looking at them for this book I had a huge, emotional surge. I really saw them anew.

This was the passing of a great man. KATE SIMON

It was like I was ordained to be with Bob Marley and The Wailers. It's like a family. It's not like I was just a cook for Bob; Bob's kids, they were like my kids. I used to take them to school. I was like their guardian more of the time. Ziggy, Steve... I'm talking about Rita's side of the family.

I've seen those kids working and they step up to the plate. I'm tellin' ya, it's no bullshit, these kids are fe real. These kids ain't playing. It's all about discipline. Just like their dad: serious. And they play soccer an' everythin'! It's like a reincarnation or something. It's like the boys have a power. Seein' these kids is just like I'm being with Bob. I like to see what they are doing; being positive, strong, defending the dynasty, no joke. No half-arsed business, these kids are fe real.
ANTONIO 'GILLIE' GILBERT

They write new songs in the spirit and with the depth of Bob. Now that is a very heavy weight. But they're up to the task. Ziggy, he's on a quest to find a new kind of music just like his father was. Same with Steven, and all of them really. They're all incredibly talented and full of passion. They have a good family spirit, and they hold each other up from what I see. They love music and the message that goes with it. STEVE JORDAN

MARLEY'S FAREWELL

Final Scenes From the Hall of the Reggae King

Fred Schruers, extracted from *The Washington Post*, May 21, 1981

It was a national wake but the mood was somehow upbeat.

Reggae king Bob Marley's body lay in state yesterday in the National Arena in Kingston, his right hand clutching a copy of the King James version of the Bible, his left hand atop the strings of a Fender Stratocaster electric guitar. He wore a denim shirt and his dreadlocks spilled out of a red, gold and green cap. An estimated 150,000 Jamaicans passed by his glass-enclosed coffin in single file during the course of the day.

Outside, Kingston's sweating constabulary conducted a tense shoving match with files of eager mourners, most of whom had waited three hours or more to pass one at a time through a checkpoint at the arena's entrance. Nearby, officers armed with semi-automatic rifles and sub-machine guns stood and waited. The police reportedly used 'chemical agents' to control a small, unruly portion of the crowd at one point, but the day passed without any bloodshed. The only incident noted was by a Kingston tabloid, *The Star*, which claimed that a photographer from the newspaper *The Gleaner* was 'manhandled' by Marley's wife Rita while attempting to photograph the arrival of the body at the airport. A family spokesman called the incident 'a misunderstandin'.

Throughout the procession there were smiles instead of tears. 'Most of these people,' said Wailers keyboardist Tyrone Downie, 'have never seen him that close'.

Marley's lying in state was the prelude to today's funeral procession by car to his home parish. After his burial at Nine Mile, the mourners will return to the National Arena where The Wailers (including Rita Marley's vocal trio The I-Three) are scheduled to perform a brief concert. Marley's mother, Cedella Booker, will also sing.

Last night in the cramped, smoky recording studio known as Tuff Gong, Booker, 54, rehearsed her song – an original composition called 'Hail' – while friends and fans sang, as they had throughout the day, their favourite Bob Marley tunes. 'I thought you were going to do "Redemption Song",' Rita Marley said to her mother-in-law. Booker agreed as The Wailers rehearsed their part in the tribute and spliffs of 'ganja' were passed into the night.

Earlier in the day, Prime Minister Edward Seaga called Marley, 'No ordinary man... a son of the ghetto who by hard work, creativity and self-discipline became a superstar. It is comforting to know that Bob Marley, Joseph of the Twelve Tribes of Israel, saw this life as but one stage in the evolution of the soul.

'Bob recently wrote a song called "I Know". Mrs Rita Marley has asked me to share with you a verse from this song: "When the race is hard to run, and you just can't stand the pace/All I know is that Jah will be waiting there, I know."'

Marley is the posthumous recipient of the Jamaica Order of Merit. Jamaica's People's National Party – Seaga's opposition – called Marley 'A champion and an apostle of justice... the musical heritage he left us is one of the treasures of this nation and his place in Jamaica's history is well assured of this. May he find the peace he so often invoked for his people.'

A spokesman for Island Records (Marley's label) in London said that worldwide sales of Marley's albums exceeded $190 million, or one-tenth of Jamaica's gross national product.

Downie, who was a close friend of Marley's, talked about the future of The Wailers without their leader: 'Everyone in the group is talented – we'll evolve into whatever we can. It's so intense right now that our whole future is based on this moment.'

There was no summing up the living Marley. The difficulty was not just his creed of Rastafarianism, which boasts some of the most tangled dogma any figure of such worldwide popularity ever sought to espouse. If his public had ever sorted out what this 36-year-old son of a white British army major and a black woman had wanted, they would have tried to give it to him. He didn't want idolatry, although he exulted in working his magnetic presence on a crowd of 18,000 in Madison Square Garden. He didn't want money; possessions embarrassed him. Perhaps he wanted most what he said he wanted most: 'For the waters of righteousness to cover the face of the earth.'

This man's reading the Bible at Bob's burial place in St Ann. I love that. The Bible's just so old... KATE SIMON

Gotta remember there's only good and bad. There's no third way. Either good or you're bad – if you're good you are Rasta, if you are bad you are Babylon. That's how it go. BOB MARLEY, 1979

He's called Tuff Gong because that man go t'ru the toughest and hardest a'time. When the music was too rugged and there was oppression and nuff people fighting as Rasta, people used to look 'pon dem [The Wailers] as rude boy in Jamaica. But Bob Marley was a hard man, believe me, unstoppable.

Him foot sick and him still out on the road. Work. That man never stop. Ya' know certain pretty things would say, 'I got a foot problem, I can't go on the road.' That man out on the road, that man a worker. JUNIOR DELGADO

I suppose it was the advent of Bob Marley when the music really transcended its island situation. That's obviously down to Chris Blackwell being there to expand on the possibilities of Marley's success. Bob Marley had it all there anyway, but maybe Chris Blackwell as a producer wanted it to happen a bit quicker.

I think as a musician, especially if you've got something to say – and that's the point – then it's any ears. There's no bias, it's for everybody to listen to, not just one select type. It's for anybody and that's crucial. You want to pass the message on. If you've got something to say, you want to pass it on. It's about communication. There's no point preaching or conversing with the converted. PAUL SIMONON

He intended to be a superstar. It wasn't a joke; he was to be a superstar. Probably was even a plan to be so. LEE 'SCRATCH' PERRY

Him get the right people around him, the right administration. Is not nothing different, jus' how him set his business, how him administrate; him have a proper manager to represent him. Most Jamaican artists don't have a manager to represent them. Most of them don't have a business.

And Bob Marley was there suffering a long time before. Until Blackwell comes along. And it's not as if when Blackwell came along he wasn't suffering.

He grows and grows and grows. Him have to do a lot of work – him and Blackwell have to do a lot of work. Not like someone just say, well you're gonna be a star overnight.

And I don't see Bob Marley as a star. Bob Marley no see himself as a star. Bob Marley is a spiritual warrior. He was a man ahead of his time. You not gonna get no more man like Bob Marley. He was a one of a kind. When him did link up with Blackwell, that was the ultimate link for Bob Marley and I have to give thanks because it was a success and it meant so much for Jamaicans and reggae music. JUNIOR DELGADO

I never used to like him [Bob Marley]. I heard all his albums like *Catch A Fire* onwards and I never could like it until I heard a bit of *Natty Dread* and *Rastaman Vibration*.

He can work with words and music; he's a genius. In that field, he is. He's done so many good songs. He's like Lennon and McCartney, you know what I mean? He's the greatest, one of the greatest.
JOE STRUMMER, 1978

Bob Marley is a man who has 'nuff reasoning ability. Progressive reasoning too, uplifting reasoning. He's a man who uplift your spirit. Very powerful man, spiritual.

And he still endure, ca' when him dead, people really start buy this man. A magic yout'.

He had a terrible yout', yet him touched the world. JUNIOR DELGADO

HAIL

FRED SCHRUERS, 2004

In the early summer of 1980 Bob Marley and The Wailers were almost midway through an extensive world tour that would take them from Libreville, Gabon to, unevocatively enough, Pittsburgh, Pennsylvania. Or unevocative Pittsburgh would seem were it not now recognisable as the last venue where Bob Marley ever took the stage. But that June, when my editor at *Rolling Stone* assigned me to join the band on a leg of their European tour, all seemed well. In fact, with the *Uprising* album having been recorded between early January concert dates in Gabon and two legendary mid-April dates in Zimbabwe, it looked to be a propitious moment in an epochal career as Bob brought his political message to an increasingly involved and enthusiastically widening public. He'd also visit Brazil that spring, hoping to tour later with Jacob Miller and Inner Circle – until Miller's untimely death in March that year, which left Bob alone (not to dismiss the rapturous and soulful work of Toots and The Maytals) at the summit of reggae music.

I knew little enough about the man, somewhat more about his music. I had interviewed him for *Circus* magazine in 1976 (coincident with a pair of dates at Manhattan's Beacon Theatre), resulting in a story not reprinted here but available to all where the sole copy I know of sits lacquered onto the wall of the Bob Marley Museum in his former home at 56 Hope Road in Kingston. On the April day of that interview, I'd turned up in the doorway of the suite he often borrowed from Island Records' Chris Blackwell. I stood uncertainly peering through a haze of blue smoke at a collection of dreadlocked and, it seemed to me at the time, hostile or sardonically amused band mates and camp followers. I recall looking at the man himself with what must have been a forlorn expression. He looked back, forehead knitted in that severely thoughtful way of his for a moment. Then came the smile that audiences often saw, as wide and beneficent as any I had ever seen. 'Hey, Skip,' he said, and patted an empty spot on the couch where he sat. That was Bob.

I would join the tour in Barcelona, where the concert took place in a bullring that was hardly as intimate as the Beacon but where he demonstrated, with a great sense of the scale of the arena and what size of gesture would reach its far corners, his unerring command of the crowd. He was exuberant on the new song 'Could You Be Loved', with its Brazilian lilt; fascinatingly querulous with an underbelly of anger as he recited the spoken interludes on 'Crazy Baldhead'; and on 'No Woman No Cry', with his hand raised to his brow, shading his eyes as he mimed an entirely believable, supplicating misery, he was completely entrancing. Any language barrier that may have existed between Marley and the cheering Spanish crowd was forgotten at such moments. The next morning I found myself talking in a car parked on a foggy side street with Tommy Cowan, a longtime football-playing pal of Bob who was as much a part of the travelling party as the band and, for that matter, the cook pots that went rattling through Europe's airports with the entourage. We were discussing Bob's Rastafarianism (he was specifically allied with the Nyahbingi tribe), and his history as the son of a white Jamaican administrator – Norval St Clair Marley, a man known as Captain who, Bob's mother Cedella would recall, 'loved to cry' – raised in a rural district in northern Jamaica but knowledgeable of the United States from his time working in an auto plant in Delaware. 'Bob,' said Tommy simply, 'Wants to speak to all the people.'

Bob was so unquestionably the centre of the travelling circus that the band, especially young and talented multi-instrumentalist Tyrone Downie, took his cue and were welcoming. They paid me the compliment of being just as stingy towards me with the ganja as they were to each other. A typical private bus transfer from the airport would feature the various band members pulling out their individual, cigar-sized, conical spliffs and drawing deeply and alone on them; any borrowing of the smoke was understood to be momentary and led to a quick, low-voiced, 'Re-turn to send-ah.' It required the introduction of a small but potent hash joint from Paris to gain any respect from the group. The advisability of such preparations before getting into a small and seemingly shaky turbo-prop plane for the flight from Nantes to Paris through a bank of slate-gray thunderheads was something they were oblivious to, although they glared silently, Rasta-style, at the weather just outside the windows that was soon rattling the plane.

What became clear upon landing was that Bob Marley and The Wailers, with a gig booked on a plain on the outskirts of Le Bourget Airport, owned the city. I had lived there for nine months, four years earlier, and watched cultural phenomena sweep through (anything Chinese was fervently embraced during that stay), but the Marley entourage, with their dreadlocks, their red, gold and green satin tour jackets and Island Records founder Chris

Blackwell languidly overseeing it all with the French actress Nathalie Delon at his side, were treated like royalty. A private boat ride down the Seine was memorable for the moment when Tyrone got in a scuffle with a local gent he thought had shown disrespect to Nathalie. The concert itself was up to the compelling Marley standard; the only time I dared duck out was during 'Three Little Birds', an amiable enough trifle which had been a regional hit in Europe. The highlight may have been the rush of the bus back into the city's centre, accompanied by the blaring klaxons of a 20-strong motorcycle escort.

Perhaps, though, the real moment of insight came in the lobby of the Hotel Nikko as the band was fitfully assembling to decamp for Dijon (and soon, London's Crystal Palace). I was saying farewell to Bob, whom I wouldn't see for almost three months, as Rita Marley and her fellow I-Three came off the elevator heading for the narrow, steep escalator that led to the street. Rita was wrestling her bulky, rolling suitcase and in a moment was in an unpromising contretemps with the escalator. There was a moment of hesitation. Bob was not a faithful husband and Rita was not an easy wife but there was much history and respect between them. With one of his easy smiles sent over his shoulder by way of goodbye, Bob Marley, Rebel Superstar, hastened as inconspicuously as possible across the lobby, wrangled the suitcase onto the escalator, and glided out of view.

The rest of the story is, of course, not happy. The band did their sweep through the British Isles and headed for America, where New York would be their base. Word came that Bob had collapsed while jogging in Central Park. He performed two nights at Madison Square Garden, and the evident energy and fire he brought to those gigs now seems heroic; perhaps he had a foreboding sense that these would truly count. The day after the second, I was scheduled to accompany Bob and the band out to the annual West Indian Day Parade in Brooklyn (where hot-blooded Jamaicans, of whom Bob would disdainfully say, 'Them too hip,' were nightly fighting it out with automatic weapons for drug territories in the rougher neighbourhoods). The plan was for the band to travel the parade route on a flatbed truck, waving and grooving to their own recordings played through a sizeable speaker set-up. I met Lister, the Island aide who had promised 'soon come' to a generation of journalists, downstairs in the Essex House lobby, and we rode up to the room with its view all the way north up Central Park to Harlem. Once again I found myself in the doorway of his suite, and again there was a smile – one I appreciated all the more because of the obvious effort it cost him. Bob was wearing one of his concert outfits, a tight denim suit with bell bottoms, but the dreadlocks he liked to unleash with a flourish were gathered under a tam and his face looked drawn. He was seated in a stiff-backed wooden chair immediately beside the door, as if he'd diligently brought himself that close before sitting back down. He seemed to be gathering himself for a moment. Finally he looked up. 'Lister,' he said, with real regret in his voice, 'Naw cyan do it.'

Bob would play that final Pittsburgh gig on September 23, 1980, and save for a brief, spoken recording (made in one of the hospitals where his life guttered out, but ostensibly sent back from a recuperative visit to Africa), he was essentially done communicating with his public in his earthly form. Except, of course, for the indispensable and enduring recordings that continue to sell and be heard throughout the world. The next time I saw him he was lying in state in a Kingston arena, Bible and guitar nestled in his arms. He had once survived an assault by gun, during the Jamaican political wars he helped to defuse, but he was mortal after all.

His body was transported, often on single lane roads, in a winding caravan to his mausoleum near his birthplace in Nine Mile in St Ann's Parish. As he was put in the tomb, I found myself as one of many white faces that had made the pilgrimage. Next to me was Chris Blackwell, certainly sombre but as usual attentive to the tenor of the assemblage, and at the same time offering comfort with personal and private grace. Afterwards, Kate Simon and I found ourselves at an impromptu memorial at Tuff Gong Studios where Cedella Booker, swaying at the centre of a small gathering of musicians, powerfully sang a hymn. We had put aside our work implements in that sacred space. As I was phoning in the story of the day's events to *The Washington Post*, I could hear the repeated, gently rocking refrain spilling through the open studio door: 'And I say, Hail, Hail, Hail...'

Later Blackwell would say of Bob's early death, 'It's a continuing sadness,' and certainly that's true. But what's proven daily and – I remember thinking one day listening to Bob's *Legend* collection play over and over in a barefoot bar called Rasta Baby II on a Thai beach – is that Bob Marley's life and music is also a continuing joy.

DREAD NO DEAD

Glenn O'Brien, *Interview* magazine, 1978

I remember when I first saw The Wailers play, in the mid-Seventies. It was their first gig in New York at Max's Kansas City. Some of us had heard the music and been moved, but to see them was something else. I remember standing with Ronnie Cutrone watching the original band, with Bob Marley, Peter Tosh and Bunny Livingston. It was revelation. Ronnie just kept uttering half under his breath, 'They're so noble! They're so noble!'

Their visual power and their musical power all seemed to spring from the spirit and it was music that moved the soul. They were rockers but they were philosophers. To me, the greatest philosophical messages of our time are in those songs.

Bob wrote: 'Some people think great God will come from the sky. Take away everything and make everybody feel high. But if you know what life is worth, you will look for yours on earth. And now you see the light, you gonna stand up for your rights.'

I recently came across interviews I did with Bob Marley and Peter Tosh at the peak of their power and their words still live. As they do. Dread no dead.

Glenn O'Brien: Do Rastas believe...

Peter Tosh: Believe? Rastas don't believe. Rastas know. There's a difference between to believe and to know. When you believe, it's 50 per cent doubt. I know things. I am not here to learn from men, but to get inspiration from the Divine Inspirator who is Jah Rastafari, who is the Creator. Because everything in these Western worlds is commercial. When a guy knows, he commercialises on what he knows and inclines to sell it. In the days of old, my father went in the Tabernacle and beat them, and said, 'My house is called a house of prayer, but thou hast made it a den of thieves.' Well, that's what's going on now. A den of pirates who call themselves learned. But he who says he knows, knows not that he doesn't know. Seen?

Glenn: Do Rastas invent new words? Like your song 'Downpressor Man', I never heard the word 'downpressor' before.

Peter: No, in the beginning was the word, man.

Glenn: So people used that word before?

Peter: Not people. People who used to exist in the time when the word was. Seen? 'Cos not everyone who is here was here. Some people just come here. And here I and I is, and will forever be. Seen? So who was here with the word still maintain the word, until this time.

Glenn: Words come from old ideas, but sometimes they change.

Peter: They change, but the original is still there. People change them by trying to add something or making them more sophisticated, or what you call modern. But the word is there. So how could there be a word called 'oppressor' [up-pressor] when to oppress mean to suck my eyes out and bury me? That's what oppression is. So how you gonna up-press down to death? Up means elevation. If I'm gonna up-press a man I'm gonna give him a couple thousand dollars, seen? If I'm gonna downpress a man, you belittle him of his rights, seen? That is downpression and that is why Babylon system is set up. That's what I tell ya about disco. Disco mean to get down. Goin' down to what? Goin' down to doom. So that's the system.

Glenn: So Rasta checks the direction of his words.

Peter: Yes, because so it was and so it shall be. Words have such psychological effect on people who don't know. A word like diet. Diet. Die it. I don't eat with them brothers there.

Glenn: Do you ever hear a word you think is wrong and correct it?

Peter: Yes, man. Yes, me have a number one dictionary of words. Yes man, serious t'ing. Like I have eliminated the word 'diet' now. Now ya go on 'live-at'. A serious thing. That's how it is to be, and it can be explained logically. Me like positive. Anything negative you try to put the positive to it to make it show light.

Glenn: I heard customs confiscated your pipe?

Peter: Ahh, this bullshit. Customs take it away and say I can't come through the customs with it, and it's my tool! Bloodclot! Talk about smoking herb, smoking herb is what the angels that dwells around inspire. Me do what me have to do. What is lawful and what you would call Godly and righteous. And you must come smoke a thing where him write upon every pack, 'Warning: the Surgeon General warns you that smoking is dangerous, it is a hazard to your health.' You must order twenty-five pack and smoke it every bumbaclot day. Bloodclot! Anything that's progress, they hold it back. That's why Jah say, 'this time I shall not come like no lamb to no slaughter or no sheep to no shearer, but terrible and dreadful, that when a guy hears my name, Ras Tafari.' The prefix 'Ras' means head, and the suffix 'Tafari' means creator. Put them together it means 'Head Creator'. He is He from such time, It is He who shall return in this time in like manner, and so terrible that when Him talk, man, all the earth tremble, when Him laugh rain fall. That's why don't do me tell about them crucify Christ, about God dead, about His Imperial Majesty dead. All that big bloodclot propaganda, well planned to make the weak weaker and the strong stronger. No gunshot can stop Ras Tafari. No ballistic missiles can stop him. 'Cos my father is the man, in the earth that the man stand on with his ballistic missile.

Man, they tell you god is a spirit. He's a living man with flesh and blood in him. It's so incredible, it's true, it's a living man doing all these things. That's why I have to praise him. 'Cos it is Him that make me after His own likeness and image, seen? And so it was, so shall it be. He still makes men in His likeness and image. But Babylon come to tell you God is a spirit and that to worship Him, you must worship Him in spirit. I am not a spirit.

Glenn: No, flesh and blood.

Peter: Ya man, that's why me stay very close to me Father. So when Him start to rock the earth, me can dance to the bloodclot rhythm. And we'll see who can dance! Fuck! So it go, yes!

Glenn: Do you believe in astrology, Bob?

Bob Marley: No Rasta! I believe in the Twelve Tribes of Israel, which them change and call astrology. Astrology is up there. And them say that God is up there. Seen? But where them get astrology from, and the ideas of astrology is from the Twelve Tribes of Israel, which every man have by tendency. Not by Roman god, but by the sons of Jacob. So man may find him root. Plenty people say, 'I'm Aquarius.' A Roman god. But you check Jacob's 12 sons and you find the tendencies. Which month ya born?

Glenn: March.

Bob: So, ya's a Benjamin. You come from the tribe of Benjamin. Ya rule the feet. There's 12 parts of the body, one for each tribe. You control the foot, you come from the tribe of Benjamin. Me come from the tribe of Joseph, that rules the leg. Now they would say me is an Aquarius. What them say ye is?

Glenn: Pisces.

Bob: Them say ye is Pisces. But if me is Aquarius and ye is Pisces and me want to check out now our roots, how can we check out roots of Pisces and Aquarius? You need a root, seen? But we know the sons of God and we check out Jacob's 12 sons, and one of the 12 we carry what them carry. Man is a universe. The eye alone can tell you that. By your eye, behold all things. But your eye cannot look within ya, ya know? So them say you must look out there. Them trick ya. God never make it so. God is within you. That means your mind control your eye. Your mind control everything. Astrology wrong in the sense of the roots, how them carry down. Maybe them purposely do it, maybe them don't purposely do it. But the Bible is the proof.

Glenn: Have the Rastas ever translated the Bible?

Bob: We don't need to translate it. We just read it and understand it. 'In the beginning God created the Heaven and the Earth, and the Earth was without form and void; and darkness was upon the face of the deep. And the Spirit of the God moved upon the face of the waters. And God said, Let there be light: and there was light.' Seen? And it go on forever continually like that, till them say them crucify God, and Him says He shall return as King of Kings, Lord of Lords, Conqueror and Lion of Judah, Alpha and Omega, you know? One man come with these names and the name is Haile Selassie. Him is the only King of Kings, Lord of Lords, Conqueror and Lion of the Tribe of Judah. The Bible say when Christ return he will return in this kingly character. So we don't need to translate the Bible, 'cos the Bible state it. And what's so nice about it is that the white man have to accept the truth of what is written in the Bible. Because his King James said, 'Yes, this Bible can go out.' Even the white man cannot deny Ras Tafari is God.

Glenn: What do you think about reincarnation?

Bob: I think when you're doing one thing you can reincarnate. But when you know good and evil, no reincarnation, because you can live forever, continually. 'Cos God have the power to do what he do.

Glenn: Once you realise good and evil you don't have to reincarnate?

Bob: When you know good and evil you don't reincarnate no more. If you do good you live forever and if you do evil you must die. And when you die you return as a dog and a bus lick ya down in the street, and ya return as a frog and a car run over ya, and ya return as a fly and somebody kill ya, and ya return as a bird and perch up on the electric and get shocked. If ya don't do the right thing, but if you do the right thing you can live forever.

Glenn: What do good men come back as?

Bob: Good men no die. Every good man live. If him get killed him do something to get killed. In a sense, some of them is just sacrifices, but them make more experienced.

Glenn: Do you think you've lived before?

Bob: Yeah.

Glenn: Do you have any idea what you were before?

Bob: Yeah, Joseph. As it was in the beginning, so shall it be in the end. In the beginning I am from the tribe of Joseph. And that is why I tell ya about the 12 sons of Jacob and not astrology. Because that's how I realised who I was in the beginning. All the amount of people on the earth is only 12 people, you know? There are only 12 different minds, 12 different tendencies. Them have their own way of doing things, because God create that. But the official man you now is Benjamin. Your tendency is Benjamin and you cannot be nothing but Benjamin, seen?

Glenn: Have you ever seen a UFO, Bob?

Bob: You ever seen one?

Glenn: No.

Bob: Me never ever see one. America can make one. Russia can make it. China can make it. They can make one of those land some little place and some people see it and them run, go way and say they seen this land. That's an illusion. That's in the spirit of madness.

'I Jesus have sent mine angel to testify unto you these things in the churches. I am the root and the offspring of David and the bright morning star. And the Spirit and the bride say "Come." And let him that heareth say "Come." And let him that is athirst say "Come." And whosoever will, let him take the water of life freely. For I testify unto every man that heareth the words of prophesy of this book, if any man shall add unto thee things, God shall add unto his the plagues that are written in this book. And if any man shall take away from the words of the book of this prophesy, God shall take away his part out of the book of life, and out of the holy city and from the things which are written in this book. He which testifieth these things saith, "Surely I come quickly. A-man. Even so, come, Jah Rastafari..."'

There is no illusion man. This is prophesy. All of these impossible things which they say man can make... they say man go to the moon. That's a little mechanical thing, man, a little glider. It's in Genesis 49: 'Benjamin shall ravin as a wolf: in the morning he shall divide the prey, and at night he shall divide the spoil.' What does 'ravin' mean?

Glenn: To prowl around, I guess.

Bob: Sayest ye! That's what you do.

Glenn: I guess Benjamin is a reporter.

Bob: Seen. So they take this and build astrology. They call it astrology, but it's Ras Tafari. It's through the laws of mankind. You can tell the tendencies from when they were born.

Glenn: What happens to the tribes in Revelation, in the Apocalypse?

Bob: Twelve thousand gather of each tribe... and a multitude a man couldn't count follow after. 144,000 people is the full strength of God. When these 144,000 people come together with the one Ras Tafari, then all of the rest of the people come together.

Glenn: After Revelation, are we still going to have electric guitars and motorcycles and Bionic Dread?

Bob: If ya want! But you don't promise it this time. If ya want a bicycle ya don't give your heart for it. Seen?

Glenn: Seen.

For me, Bob Marley resides in the pantheon alongside of Dylan, Elvis Presley, James Brown and Woody Guthrie. He is one of the few musicians who can truly be described as revolutionary. He made music that ministered simultaneously to the body, soul and mind. He filled your spirit, made you dance and sharpened your thoughts. His reach went far beyond the world of music – into the lives and struggles of those he inspired. He was without a doubt one of the greatest writers of socially conscious music of the second half of the century. His early death remains an incalculable loss, not just to music, but to the world at large.

BRUCE SPRINGSTEEN, 2004

Rock and roll is the universal language.
I thought.
It's not.
I mean, it travels OK. Like jazz does, like salsa, like doo-wop, whatever.

Once one travels to the deepest darkest jungles of Africa, the mountaintops of Tibet, the Buddhist temples of Southeast Asia, and the canals of Amsterdam, it becomes obvious. There is only one King of Cultural Common Ground.

From the purity of young romance, to the uncompromising commitment of revolution, and every emotion in between, no voice has ever spoken such transcendent truth with such universal authority and communicated it so effectively.

The sheer breadth of the content of his work is impressive on its own (he covered the spectrum socially, politically, sexually and spiritually), but it is the consistently high quality of the records and live performances that is staggering.

The other Wailers, Peter and Bunny, his band, and producers deserve equally high praise and recognition as irreplaceable members of his family and essential to his success.

It will be many generations before music again produces an artist so respected and beloved worldwide as Bob Marley. STEVEN VAN ZANDT, 2004

I was hanging in Jamaica in '72 after the *Goats Head Soup* sessions. There was a feeling in the air. I went to the record store to find out what there was. I walked out with *The Harder they Come* and *Catch a Fire* and I realised this was more than a feeling.

Jamaica was bursting with talent and originality. Bob Marley, Jimmy Cliff, Kenny Boothe and Eric Donaldson were everywhere. It reminded me of the atmosphere in England in '63 when The Beatles and The Stones were changing the face of pop music.

Reggae rhythm and a unique sense of melody turned Jamaica into a musical powerhouse. I never got over it and later I had the great experience of working with Sly Dunbar and Robbie Shakespeare as well as with the one and only Lee 'Scratch' Perry on 'Heavy Voodoo'.

It would be a sin not to mention the one and only Gregory Isaacs, Jacob Miller and Toots Hibbert among so many other great talents that Jamaica has given birth to.

No one will ever forget the impact Bob and Jamaican music had on the world.

ONE LOVE!

KEITH RICHARDS

TIMELINE

CHRONOLOGY OF RECORDINGS & UK/US RELEASES

1945

6 February - Robert Nesta Marley is born in Nine Mile, a small rural community in the mountainside parish of St Ann, Jamaica. His mother, Cedella Malcolm (then Marley, then Booker) is 18 years old and deeply in love with Bob's father, the 50-something Norval Marley, a white Jamaican. The difference in both age and skin colour, and, most importantly, the resulting pressure from Norval Marley's family, mean Bob will see precious little of his father and his parents will never live together.

1950

Now separated from Cedella, Norval convinces his former wife that their son should travel to Kingston where he will pay for his schooling. With some reluctance, Cedella agrees.

1951

Bob returns to Nine Mile almost 18 months after leaving. Bob has not seen his father since he was picked up at the bus station in Kingston and dispatched to live with an elderly lady for whom he runs errands. It is while at a fruit market one day that a friend of Cedella's from Nine Mile spots the young boy. Cedella promptly dashes to Kingston to fetch him.

1956

Taddeus (Toddy) Livingston and his son Neville move to Nine Mile. Neville - or Bunny as he is more commonly known - becomes Bob's closest friend. Their relationship is forged on a shared interest in music and further strengthened when Cedella and Taddeus move in together.

1961

Having moved to Trench Town with his mother, Taddeus and Bunny, Bob finishes his schooling. Aged 15, he takes a job as an apprentice welder, but spends most of his time with Bunny learning the musical arts under the tutelage of singer Joe Higgs through informal, but nevertheless intense lessons. It is around this time that Bunny and Bob meet Winston McIntosh (later Peter Tosh) who is one of the few people in the tenement yards to actually own an instrument, a somewhat battered guitar.

1962

Bob seeks out a young Jimmy Cliff who, at this time, is working for producer Leslie Kong as an A&R man. Jimmy Cliff likes what he hears and subsequently Bob records four tracks for Kong: 'Judge Not', 'Do You Still Love Me', 'Terror' and 'One More Cup Of Coffee'.

LESLIE KONG PRODUCTIONS FOR THE BEVERLEY'S LABEL:

Do You Still Love Me / Judge Not — As Robert Marley
One More Cup Of Coffee — As Bobby Marten
Terror — As yet unreleased

1963

The Wailing Wailers are formed drawing the best from Joe Higgs's informal talent school. It comprises Bob Marley, Bunny Livingston, Peter Tosh, Junior Braithwaite, Beverley Kelso and Cherry Green. Another musical mentor and friend of Higgs's, Alvin 'Seeco' Patterson, takes them to audition for leading ska producer Clement 'Sir Coxsone' Dodd. In the final weeks of the year, renamed The Wailers, they release their first single for Studio One, 'Simmer Down'.

CLEMENT 'SIR COXSONE' DODD PRODUCTIONS FOR HIS STUDIO ONE LABEL:

Christmas Is Here / Climb The Ladder / Destiny / Do You Remember / I Don't Need Your Love / I'm Going Home / Mr Talkative / Simmer Down / Straight And Narrow / Tell Them Lord / Your Love

1964

'Simmer Down' goes to Number One in the Jamaican charts where it stays for two months, reportedly selling around 80,000 copies, a staggering number for an island with a population of little more than 1.6million. The song addresses the gangs of 'rude boys' emerging in the ghettos. Unfortunately, the warning will go unheeded and gang violence, fuelled by poverty and unscrupulous politicians, will continue to escalate.

The Wailers go on recording a steady stream of hits with the legendary Skatalites as backing band. Though the hottest group on the island, they earn just £3 a week each in wages. Bob does further work for Coxsone picking through piles of American import singles for use on his sound system. He also helps audition and coach new talent, including a trio called The Soulettes featuring a young Rita Anderson.

CLEMENT 'SIR COXSONE' DODD PRODUCTIONS FOR HIS STUDIO ONE LABEL:

Amen / Dance With Me / Don't Ever Leave Me / Donna / Go Jimmy Go / Habits / Hoot Nanny Hoot / I Made A Mistake / I Need You / It Hurts To Be Alone / Lonesome Feelings / Love Won't Be Mine This Way / Maga Dog / Nobody Knows / Oh My Darling / Teenager In Love / There She Goes / True Confessions / Where Will I Find / Wings Of A Dove

1965

Beverley Kelso quits the band, allegedly tired of Bob's relentless perfectionism. Junior Braithwaite having left for America the year before, The Wailers trim themselves down to a core trio of Bob, Bunny and Peter. The hits keep coming with early recordings of 'One Love' and 'Rude Boy' sitting next to some seemingly odd (with hindsight at least) cover versions like The Beatles' 'And I Love Her' and Tom Jones' 'What's New Pussycat'.

At the end of the year, The Wailers' dominance of the Jamaican charts is confirmed when they have five records in the Top Ten at the same time.

CLEMENT 'SIR COXSONE' DODD PRODUCTIONS FOR HIS STUDIO ONE LABELS:

And I Love Her / Another Dance / Cry To Me / Diamond Baby / Do It Right / Do You Feel The Same Way Too / Good Good Rudie / Guajira Ska / Hooligans / I Left My Sins / I'm Gonna Put It On / I'm Still Waiting / Jumbie Jamboree / Just In Time / Let The Lord Be Seen In You / Lonesome Track / Love And Affection / One Love / Playboy / Rude Boy / Shame And Scandal / Ska Jerk / Somewhere To Lay My Head / Ten Commandments Of Love / The Jerk / This Train / Wages Of Love / What's New Pussycat / Where Is My Mother / Where's The Girl For Me / White Christmas

UK RELEASES:

January: 'Simmer Down / I Don't Need Your Love' — through Ska Beat
March: 'It Hurts To Be Alone / Mr Talkative' — through Island
April: 'Playboy / Your Love'
May: 'Hoot Nanny Hoot / Do You Remember' — A-side credited to Peter Touch, B-side Bob Marley
May: 'Hooligans / Maga Dog'
June: 'Shame And Scandal / The Jerk'
June: 'Don't Ever Leave Me / Donna'
August: 'Lonesome Feelings / There She Goes'
October: 'I Made A Mistake'
December: 'What's New Pussycat / Where Will I Find'

1966

Due to the nature of the Jamaican music industry – which in the Sixties makes serfdom seem fair – The Wailers are now the biggest group on the island but still struggling financially. At the end of 1965, Coxsone had paid them a scant £99 bonus for almost single-handedly making him the richest producer in Jamaica. It becomes clear to The Wailers that the only way to make serious money from music is to produce it and own it, but they lack the funds to set up their own label.

Bob's mother is now living in Delaware, USA, where she has married a man named Edward Booker. She sends Bob the air ticket to join her. On 10 February, Bob marries Rita Anderson, supposedly on the advice of Coxsone who points out that if he wants to stay in the US, it's easier to get a visa for a wife than a girlfriend. The next day (some suggest it's actually a few days later), Bob leaves Jamaica for the US leaving his bride behind.

Peter and Bunny continue to record with Rita's cousin, Constantine 'Dream' (or 'Vision') Walker, and occasionally Rita. Following Haile Selassie I's visit to Jamaica in April, The Wailers become committed Rastafarians and start to 'locks up'. Bob returns to the island in October and 'sights' Rasta too.

Thanks to his work at the Chrysler car factory in Wilmington, Delaware, the group now have enough money to set up their label, which they call Wail 'N Soul 'M. Their first single is a clear message to Coxsone Dodd: it's titled 'Freedom Time'.

CLEMENT 'SIR COXSONE' DODD PRODUCTIONS FOR HIS STUDIO ONE LABEL:

Blowing In The Wind / Can't You See / Dancing Shoes / Don't Look Back / Dreamland / He Who Feels It Knows It / I Need You / I Stand Predominant / Jerking Time / Lemon Tree / Let Him Go / Little Boy Blue / Making Love / Rasta Shook Them Up / Rock Sweet Rock / Rolling Stone / Sentimental Journey / Sinner Man / Sunday Morning / The Toughest / Treat Me Good / What Am I Supposed To Do / When The Well Runs Dry — these recordings all made without Bob who spends most of '66 in Delaware. His position is taken by Constantine Walker; Bend Down Low / Freedom Time

UK RELEASES:

March: 'Jumbie Jamboree' — through Island

April: 'Put It On / Love Won't Be Mine'

November: 'He Who Feels It Knows It / Sunday Morning'

December: 'Let Him Go / Sinner Man'

Some sources list the following single releases for this year with no specific dates:

Love And Affection / And I Love Her / Lonesome Track / Dancing Shoes / Rude Boy / Good Good Rudie / Rasta Put It On — through Ska Beat, Rio and Doctor Bird

1967

Opening a small record store in Kingston, The Wailers struggle to make their new label financially viable. Bob delivers records around the island on his bicycle. The group have a series of moderate hits but are set back when Bunny is jailed for possession of marijuana from June 1967 to September 1968. The label will eventually fold.

Around this time, American soul singer Johnny Nash and his business partners Arthur Jenkins and Danny Sims relocate to Jamaica. Danny Sims has been at the forefront of the black civil rights struggle in the US and has been promoting black artists in the Caribbean – as well as booking lectures by Malcolm X in the US – for some time. Nash sees Bob perform at a Rasta grounation and recommends him to Sims. Soon Bob is signed to a writing contract by the trio's JAD label (Johnny, Arthur and Danny). Bob is obsessed with the desire to have a hit on the US R&B charts.

SELF-PRODUCED FOR THE WAILERS' OWN WAIL 'N SOUL 'M LABEL:

Bus Dem Shut / Freedom Time / Funeral / Hammer / Hypocrites / Lyrical Satyrical / Mellow Mood / Nice Time / Pound Get Blow / Stir It Up / Thank You Lord / This Train

UK RELEASES:

April: 'I Need You' — through Island

April: 'I Am The Toughest'

Some sources list the following releases for this year with no specific dates:

I Stand Predominant — through Studio One

1968

Bob begins to record for JAD and the tracks are sent to New York for re-touching by members of Aretha Franklin's backing band. Most of these recordings were only recently released in the JAD 12-CD series *The Complete Bob Marley And The Wailers 1967–1972*.

Between 1967 and 1969, The Wailers frequently return to the hills of Nine Mile, living like simple farmers to escape the tensions of Kingston as Bob fights writer's block.

SELF-PRODUCED FOR THE WAILERS' OWN WAIL 'N SOUL 'M LABEL:

Chances Are / Dem A Fi Get A Beatin' / Don't Rock My Boat / Fire Fire / I'm Hurting Inside / Play Play Play / Stepping Razor / The Lord Will Make A Way

PRODUCED BY ARTHUR JENKINS AND JOE VENNERI FOR JAD RECORDS:

Bend Down Low / Chances Are / Fallin' In And Out Of Love / Gonna Get You / Hammer / How Many Times / It Hurts To Be Alone / Lonely Girl / Lonesome Feelings / Mellow Mood / Milk Shake And Potato Chips / Nice Time / Put It On / Rock Steady / Soul Almighty / Soul Rebel / Splish For My Splash / Stay With Me / Stranger On The Shore / The World Is Changing / There She Goes / Touch Me / Treat You Right / What Goes Around Comes Around / You Think I Have No Feelings / You Say I Have No Feelings (alternate version)

PRODUCED BY MORTIMER PLANNO:

A Little Prayer / Selassie Is The Chapel

UK RELEASES:

October: 'Stir It Up / This Train' — through Trojan

1969

Johnny Nash scores an international hit with 'Comma Comma', written by Bob Marley.

SELF-PRODUCED BY THE WAILERS:

Feel Alright / Rhythm / Tread On

PRODUCED BY TED POWDER:

Adam And Eve / Thank You Lord / This Train / Wisdom

1970

In the spring, The Wailers record an album with Leslie Kong. The producer, who has become rich through hits like 'The Israelites' and Millie Small's 'My Boy Lollipop', insists on calling it *The Best Of The Wailers*. Bunny points out that you can't know one's best until the end of one's life, and since The Wailers are so young and fit and unlikely to die any time soon, it must mean Kong is. Kong ignores the warning, releases the album and promptly dies.

Later the same year, The Wailers join up with Lee 'Scratch' Perry and record what many believe to be the best work of their career. Joining with the best rhythm section on the island – Aston 'Family Man' Barrett and his brother Carlton, 'The Upsetters' – they record classics like '400 Years', 'Soul Rebel', 'Kaya', 'Mr Brown' and 'African Herbsman'. Although the band and their eccentric producer have agreed to split all royalties 50-50, Perry allegedly sells the tapes to the Trojan label in England. They are released as the albums *Soul Rebels*, *African Herbsman* and *Soul Revolution Parts I and II*. The Wailers never received a penny in royalties from these recordings until *The Complete Wailers* series began in 1996.

PRODUCED BY LESLIE KONG:

Baby Baby Come Home / Back Out / Can't You See / Caution / Cheer Up / Do It Twice / Go Tell It On The Mountain / Soon Come / Sophisticated Psychedelication / Soul Captives / Soul Shakedown Party / Stop The Train

SELF-PRODUCED BY THE WAILERS:

Black Progress / Comma Comma / Hold On To This Feeling / Oppressor Man / The Letter / Trouble Dub / Trouble On The Road Again / High Tide Or Low Tide

PRODUCED BY RANDY'S:

Sugar Sugar / Field Marshall No Parshall

Hold On To This Feeling — by Bob and Rita

PRODUCED BY LEE 'SCRATCH' PERRY:

400 Years / Axe Man / Corner Stone / Duppy Conqueror / It's Alright / Jah Is Mighty / Long Long Winter / Man To Man / My Cup / No Sympathy / No Water / Picture On The Wall / Put It On / Reaction / Rebel's Hop / Run For Cover / Shocks Of Mighty / Small Axe / Soul Almighty / Soul Rebel / Try Me

PRODUCED BY BUNNY LEE:

Mr Chatterbox / No Love

UK RELEASES:

September: 'Soul Shakedown Party' — through Trojan

December: *Soul Rebels*

December: 'Duppy Conqueror' — through Upsetter

1971

Understandably angry at being ripped off for the second time in their career, The Wailers have another go at setting up their own label. Called Tuff Gong after Bob's nickname, it is managed by his best friend, the footballer Allan 'Skill' Cole. They get a measure of revenge on Lee 'Scratch' Perry by persuading his rhythm section, the Barrett brothers, to join them. Producing themselves, The Wailers enjoy a second run of local hits, which include 'Screw Face', 'Trench Town Rock', 'Concrete Jungle', 'Lively Up Yourself' and 'Guava Jelly'. The latter will also be successfully covered by Barbra Streisand and Johnny Nash, who also has a hit with Bob's 'Stir It Up'.

Bob spends much of the year living in Sweden where he is helping Johnny Nash write the soundtrack to a film in which he is starring – *Vill Så Gärna Tro*. The film flops, and only two of Bob's instrumental recordings make the soundtrack.

PRODUCED BY LEE 'SCRATCH' PERRY:

African Herbsman / All In One / Brainwashing / Brand New Secondhand / Downpressor / Dreamland / Fussing And Fighting / In The Iway / Kaya / Keep On Moving / Keep On Skanking / Memphis / Riding High / Stand Alone / Turn Me Loose / Who Is Mister Brown

CO-PRODUCED BY LEE 'SCRATCH' PERRY AND THE WAILERS:

Don't Rock My Boat / I Like It Like This / Love Light / Send Me That Love / Sun Is Shining

SELF-PRODUCED BY THE WAILERS:

Back Biter / Concrete Jungle / Craven Choke Puppy / Guava Jelly / Hammer / How Many Times / I'm Still Waiting / It Hurts To Be Alone / Lick Samba / Lively Up Yourself / Music Lesson / Redder Than Red / Rocking Steady / Satisfy My Soul Babe / Satisfy My Soul Jah Jah / Screw Face / Trench Town Rock / Why Should I

PRODUCED BY JOHNNY NASH:

Dance Do The Reggae / I'm Hurting Inside / Oh Lord I Got To Get There / Reggae On Broadway

UK RELEASES:

January: 'Mr Brown' — through Upsetter

February: 'Kaya'

February: 'Small Axe / All In One'

November: 'Trench Town Rock' — through Green Door

Some sources list the following single releases for this year with no specific dates:

Dreamland / More Axe / Picture On The Wall / Mr Chatterbox / Downpressor / Soultown / Lick Samba / Stop The Train / Lively Up Yourself — through various labels

1972

Bob goes to England with Danny Sims to support Johnny Nash's UK tour. According to Sims they played 'hundreds of shows' in schools and colleges and Bob releases the single 'Reggae On Broadway' on CBS UK.

Bob is now virtually penniless and stuck in the UK. He seeks out Chris Blackwell, a white Jamaican who owns Island Records and who has graduated from releasing Jamaican recordings (including early Marley material) to handling major rock acts like Traffic. Blackwell sees a chance to market The Wailers as a rock group and expand their audience beyond Jamaica to the album-buying rock audience. He gives Bob, Bunny and Peter £8,000 to record an album. *Catch A Fire* is finished less than a month later.

SELF-PRODUCED BY THE WAILERS:

400 Years / All Day All Night / Concrete Jungle / Kinky Reggae / Midnight Ravers / No More Trouble / Pass It On / Rock It Babe / Slave Driver / Stir It Up / Stop That Train

UK RELEASES:

May: 'Reggae On Broadway / Oh Lord I Got To Get There' — through CBS

September: 'Keep On Moving / African Herbsman' — through Trojan

Some sources list the following single releases for this year with no specific dates:

Guava Jelly / Screw Face

1973

Catch A Fire gets the full rock treatment. Under Chris Blackwell's direction, subtle overdubs are made to tracks in London, including a slide guitar part on 'Concrete Jungle'. The record is packaged in a unique cover that looks like a giant Zippo lighter and receives good critical reviews, if not the sales to match. However, there's enough interest from the rock status quo for The Wailers play the BBC's flagship music show *The Old Grey Whistle Test* in the UK, and open for Bruce Springsteen during his residency at the legendary Max's Kansas City bar in New York.

A follow-up album, *Burnin',* is released at the end of the year and The Wailers find themselves dividing all their time between studio sessions and live work. Unhappy with what he sees as scant financial reward for their efforts, Bunny quits the group in the spring, returns to Jamaica and vows never to stray into Babylon again.

Their old mentor Joe Higgs joins Peter and Bob for an American tour in support of Sly and The Family Stone. The band last just five shows having struggled to connect with Sly's audience.

At the end of the year, Peter Tosh quits the group too.

SELF-PRODUCED BY THE WAILERS:

Burnin' And Lootin' / Duppy Conqueror / Get Up Stand Up / Hallelujah Time / I Shot The Sheriff / Iron Lion Zion / No Sympathy / One Foundation / Pass It On / Put It On / Rastaman Chant / Reincarnated Soul / Small Axe

UK & US RELEASES:

April: 'Stop That Train / Baby We've Got A Date' — all now through Island

April: *Catch A Fire*

June: 'Concrete Jungle / Reincarnated Soul' (UK only)

July: 'Concrete Jungle / No More Trouble' (US only)

September: 'Get Up Stand Up / Slave Driver'

November: *Burnin'*

1974

With the original Wailers now in disarray, Bob retains the Barrett brothers as his rhythm section and recruits three established female singers. Marcia Griffiths, Judy Mowatt and Rita Marley have all had individual success in Jamaica and are almost a band within a band, calling themselves The I-Three. Al Anderson also joins the line-up; a US-based rock guitarist, his addition is a sign that Bob is aiming to expand the dynamics of reggae music.

PRODUCED BY BOB MARLEY AND THE WAILERS:

Am A Do / Belly Full / Bend Down Low / Natty Dread / Lively Up Yourself / Rebel Music / Revolution / Road Block / So Jah Seh / Talking Blues

UK & US RELEASES:

February: 'I Shot The Sheriff / Put It On' (US only)

1975

Natty Dread, the band's first album under their new name, Bob Marley and The Wailers, is the international breakthrough Bob has waited so long for. It reaches Number Ninety-Two in the US in May 1975 and Number Forty-Three in the UK the following October.

Bob's rise to stardom gets a welcome shot in the arm in July when Eric Clapton takes a version of Bob's 'I Shot The Sheriff' (from *Burnin'*) to Number One in the US and Number Nine in the UK.

Peter Tosh starts his own label, Intel-Diplo HIM (Intelligent Diplomat for His Imperial Majesty).

Old friend Alvin 'Seeco' Patterson joins the band on percussion, and Tyrone Downie on keyboards.

Bob tours to promote *Natty Dread*. Highlights include a series of dates at the Lyceum Ballroom in London – where the album *Live!* is recorded – and a show at LA's Roxy Theatre attended by such high-ranking members of the rock aristocracy as George Harrison, Ringo Starr and Bob Dylan.

By the end of the year, Bob has begun his elevation from mere rock star to someone whose words carry political and spiritual weight around the world. His position is reinforced with songs like 'War'. Basing its lyrics on a 1968 speech Haile Selassie gave to the United Nations, the song proclaims: 'Until the philosophy which holds one race/Superior and another inferior/Is finally and permanently discredited and abandoned/Everywhere is war, me say war.'

In October, the live single 'No Woman No Cry' – recorded at the Lyceum – goes to Number Twenty-Two in the UK charts followed in December by the album *Live!*, which goes to Number Thirty-Eight.

PRODUCED BY BOB MARLEY AND THE WAILERS:

Crazy Baldhead / Cry To Me / I Know / Johnny Was / Night Shift / Positive Vibration / Rat Race / Roots, Rock, Reggae / Want More / War / Who The Cap Fit

CO-PRODUCED BY BOB MARLEY AND THE WAILERS AND LEE PERRY:

Jah Live

UK & US RELEASES:

May: *Natty Dread* (UK 43, US 92)
June: 'Natty Dread / So Jah Seh' (UK only)
June: 'Lively Up Yourself / So Jah Seh' (US only)
August: 'No Woman No Cry / Kinky Reggae' (UK 22)
December: *Live!* (UK 38, US 90)

1976

Rastaman Vibration is released in April and goes to Number Eight in the US – Bob's only US top ten success – and Number Fifteen in the UK. Packaged in a unique hessian-sack cloth covering designed by Neville Garrick, it sells millions worldwide. The band tour Europe to promote it.

Bob suggests a free concert for the people of Jamaica, but insists to Prime Minister Michael Manley that it should be free of all political connotations. Manley agrees. The concert is announced for Sunday 5 December in Kingston's Heroes Park. Mere days after the announcement, Manley declares national elections to be held just weeks after the concert, making Bob's gesture of goodwill to the people appear – to some at least – an endorsement of the prime minister's political ambitions. He begins to receive death threats.

On 3 December, gunmen break into Bob's home at 56 Hope Road and start shooting. Bob's manager, Don Taylor, is hit several times in the groin and loses so much blood he is at first thought to be dead. Rita is hit in the head and a bullet grazes Bob's chest and lodges in his arm.

Bob takes sanctuary at Chris Blackwell's hilltop residence, Strawberry Hill, surrounded by armed members of Rastafarian sect the Twelve Tribes of Israel. After much deliberation Bob decides, at the very last moment, that the concert will go ahead.

Many of The Wailers have fled the island, but Bob is whisked down from the mountains under armed guard and plays an emotionally charged set. As a finale, he displays his wounds to the crowd then points his fingers like pistols at the audience before leaving the stage. Immediately he and Neville Garrick take Chris Blackwell's private jet to Nassau. Weeks later they fly on again to London. Bob will not return to Jamaica for 14 months.

CO-PRODUCED BY BOB MARLEY AND THE WAILERS AND LEE PERRY:

Smile Jamaica (Parts I and II)

UK & US RELEASES:

January: 'Jah Live / Concrete Jungle' (UK only)
April: 'Johnny Was / Cry To Me' (UK only)
April: *Rastaman Vibration* (UK 15, US 8)
June: 'Roots Rock Reggae / Stir It Up' (UK only)
June: 'Roots Rock Reggae / Cry To Me' (US 51)
November: 'Who The Cap Fit' (US only)

1977

Bob and the rest of The Wailers spend much of the year living in a house on Oakley Street, London. Here, Bob enjoys a purple patch in his writing, perfecting songs that will later appear on *Exodus* and *Kaya*. The former is released in May (June in the US) and will go to Number Eight in the UK and Number Twenty in the US.

British-based guitarist Junior Marvin joins the band. His occasional rock-style solos initially upset reggae purists, but are encouraged by Bob.

Bob and The Wailers embark on what should be the biggest reggae tour in history. It begins in Paris where, as happens at nearly all their tour dates, the band play a local team at football. In this case, it's a team of French journalists, one of whom is wearing studded boots when he steps on Bob's foot. His big toe is badly injured, the toenail bloodied, and he is taken to hospital. It is here that doctors first spot what they think is a melanoma on his toe.

Despite the injury, Marley continues the tour, and the football matches, wearing bandages and sandals. Other than these, there is no sign that he is in serious pain. However, upon finishing the European leg with a legendary string of dates at London's Rainbow Theatre, the rest of the tour is cancelled at the end of June. Part of his toe is removed in the hope that this will stop the cancer's spread.

In December, the double-A side single 'Jamming'/'Punky Reggae Party' is released in the UK. The country's punks have wholeheartedly embraced reggae; Stiff Little Fingers cover Bob's 'Johnny Was' and The Clash consistently fuse elements of reggae into their music. Bob was initially sceptical of these 'crazy baldheads' but the single signified his acceptance of them. It goes to Number Nine the following year.

PRODUCED BY BOB MARLEY AND THE WAILERS:

Crisis / Easy Skanking / Every Need Got An Ego To Feed / Exodus / Guiltiness / Is This Love / Jamming / Kaya / Misty Morning / Natural Mystic / One Love/People Get Ready / Roots / Running Away / Satisfy My Soul / She's Gone / So Much Things To Say / Sun Is Shining / The Heathen / Three Little Birds / Time Will Tell / Turn Your Lights Down Low / Waiting In Vain

PRODUCED BY LEE PERRY:

Who Colt The Game (unissued) / I Know A Place Where We Can Carry On (unissued) / Keep On Moving / Natural Mystic / Punky Reggae Party / Rainbow Country

UK & US RELEASES:

May: *Exodus* (UK 8, US 20)
June: 'Exodus / Exodus Dub' (UK 14)
August: 'Waiting In Vain / Roots' (UK 27)
December: 'Jamming / Punky Reggae Party' (UK 9)

1978

In March, *Kaya* is released to mixed reviews. The album is less militant than previous releases and features spliffed-out mellow tunes like 'Easy Skanking', 'Time Will Tell' and 'Satisfy My Soul'. The softening in mood is reflected in Neville Garrick's artwork – an adaptation of Kate Simon's warm portrait of Bob with a wide grin across his face. It will go to Number Four in the UK and Number Fifty in the US.

Still living in London, Bob is approached by rival gunmen from Kingston's ghettoes. Jamaica's warring political parties had long been playing the gangs off against each other, effectively employing them as private armies. Sharing a prison cell, two gunmen – Claude Massop and Bucky Marshall – decide they'd actually be better off calling a truce.

They do so and to mark it propose a massive concert for April 22, the 12th anniversary of Haile Selassie's visit to Jamaica. They want Bob to headline the event. Despite intial fears for his safety, he agrees.

He is the final performer of an eight-hour concert that includes an incendiary performance by Peter Tosh who harangues the assembled politicians under a thunderous sky. Bob takes a less confrontational – though no less courageous – approach. He insists the two rival political leaders, Prime Minister Michael Manley and Edward Seaga, join him on stage. In front of 40,000 people he makes them shake hands while he dances shamanically between them.

In June, Bob receives the United Nations' Peace Medal in New York, 'on behalf of 500 million Africans'.

A summer tour sees Bob attracting his largest audiences ever. Many of the shows are recorded and released on the album *Babylon By Bus.*

Bob records nothing during '78. Instead he tours the world and oversees the completion of Tuff Gong Studios at 56 Hope Road.

UK & US RELEASES:

February: 'Is This Love / Crisis' (UK 9)
March: *Kaya* (UK 4, US 50)
May: 'Satisfy My Soul / Smile Jamaica' (UK 21)
December: *Babylon By Bus* (UK 40)

1979

Bob tours the world for much of the year, visiting such far flung places as Japan and New Zealand, where he is given a royal welcome and greeted as a hero. He becomes the first reggae act to headline at Harlem's famous Apollo Theatre and plays a benefit at Harvard Stadium in Boston to raise funds for African freedom fighters.

In October, *Survival* is released. A return to his earlier militancy, it goes to Number Twenty in the UK and Number Seventy in the US.

PRODUCED BY BOB MARLEY AND THE WAILERS:

Africa Unite / Ambush / Babylon System / Mix Up Mix Up / One Drop / Ride Natty Ride / So Much Trouble In The World / Survival / Top Rankin' / Wake Up And Live / Zimbabwe

PRODUCED BY BOB MARLEY AND THE WAILERS AND LEE PERRY:

Blackman Redemption / Rastaman Live Up

UK & US RELEASES:

July: 'Wake Up And Live' (US only)
September: 'So Much Trouble In The World' (UK 56)
October: *Survival* (UK 20, US 70)
November: 'One Drop / Kaya' (US only)
November: 'Survival / Wake Up And Live' (UK only)

1980

In January Bob performs in Africa for the first time. He is invited by the president of Gabon to play in Libreville. Bob's excitement is tempered by the fact that the concert is a private one and the general populace isn't allowed in. His second concert in Africa is under very different circumstances. He is invited to the birth of a new nation: Zimbabwe's independence celebrations. Along with Prince Charles, he watches the British flag lowered on the former colony for the last time. He plays two nights and spends around $250,000 of his own money shipping over a stage, the band and other equipment.

Uprising is released in June to ecstatic reviews. It will go to Number Six in the UK and Number Forty-Five in the US and leads to the largest concert audiences of his career. In Milan he and The Wailers play to over 100,000 people. They are said to have outdrawn the Pope who appeared in the same football stadium just a week earlier.

Despite his growing success, Bob is still desperate to reach the African-American audience who he feels aren't listening. He shares the stage with The Commodores in September at Madison Square Garden. The New York show is a sell out but the next day Bob collapses while jogging in Central Park with Danny Sims and Allan 'Skill' Cole. Doctors inform him that the melanoma detected in his foot three years earlier has spread through his body and is now running rampant in his lungs and brain. Bob is given just weeks to live. Always one to put work first, he flies to Pittsburgh to perform one final concert at the Stanley Theatre on 23 September. The last song he ever sings live is a medley of 'Work'/'Get Up, Stand Up' in which he counts down the days, finishing: 'Two days to go: working for the next day/One day to go now: working for the next day/Every day is work.' For those aware of his plight, it's a powerful, emotional statement.

He returns to New York for treatment but doctors give up hope in October. Still not prepared to admit defeat himself, he flies to Bavaria to begin treatment with a controversial ex-SS Nazi doctor named Dr Josef Issels. The treatment revolves around diet and heat treatment.

PRODUCED BY BOB MARLEY AND THE WAILERS:

Bad Card / Coming In From The Cold / Could You Be Loved / Forever Loving Jah / Give Thanks And Praises / Pimper's Paradise / Real Situation / Redemption Song / Trench Town / We And Them / Work / Zion Train

PRODUCED BY KING SPORTY:

Buffalo Soldier

UK & US RELEASES:

March: 'Zimbabwe / Survival' (UK only)
May: 'Could You Be Loved / One Drop' (UK 5)
May: 'Could You Be Loved / Ride Natty Ride' (US only)
June: *Uprising* (UK 6, US 45)
August: 'Three Little Birds / Every Need Got An Ego To Feed' (UK 17)
October: 'Redemption Song' (UK only)
November: 'Redemption Song / Coming In From The Cold' (US only)

1981

Against all odds, Bob hangs on to life for several months more. Finally, in May, Issels tells Bob and his family that there is nothing more that can be done. He flies to Miami to be with his mother. He dies on the morning of Monday 11 May.

Jamaica, and the rest of the world, is shocked. Many people, misled by early media reports that claimed Bob was merely suffering from exhaustion, had not believed he was seriously ill. Jamaica's parliament recesses for ten days and a state funeral is organised for 21 May.

The recently elected Prime Minister Edward Seaga delivers Bob's eulogy – which some find ironic given the widespread belief that it was Seaga's gunmen who shot Bob in 1976. The funeral raises further controversy when it's realised it will be an Ethiopian Orthodox Church service and not strictly Rastafarian. In response, Bob's best friend Allan 'Skill' Cole ignores strict instructions to stick to his given speech and futile attempts are made to remove him from the stage.

Members of The Wailers and The I-Three perform at the service and afterwards, and thousands line the roads to watch Bob's body being driven on the back of a blue flatbed truck to his birthplace, and final resting place, in Nine Mile, St Ann.

Recording chronology compiled by Roger Steffens. Timeline based on various sources, including Roger's website www.reggaesupersite.com

INDEX

You don't need me to come tell you no more; you have to think now. Look now. Look for yourself. Get your head above the water and enjoy yourself. BOB MARLEY, 1979

IN THE PICTURE

ASTON 'FAMILY MAN' BARRETT: See *Contributors*, page 6.

CARLTON BARRETT: Aston's brother, and the other half of reggae's most respected rhythm section and originator of the 'one drop' percussive style. Carlton was murdered in 1987.

BIG YOUTH: Perhaps the most important and influential DJ after U-Roy, Big Youth's heavy roots style became famous on such classics as *Screaming Target* and *Dread Locks Dread*.

CHRIS BLACKWELL: See *Contributors*, page 6.

DENNIS BROWN: Often referred to as The Crown Prince of Reggae, Dennis enjoyed a long string of hits in the Seventies recording for Joe Gibbs. He died in 1999.

ERROL BROWN: Became senior engineer at Tuff Gong Studios following an acclaimed apprenticeship with his uncle Duke Reid and later Sonia Pottinger.

BURNING SPEAR: Enjoyed the biggest international impact after Bob Marley with his chant-like, hypnotic music. He remains a compelling performer.

COUNTRYMAN: Simple fisherman with deeply spiritual ideals. *Rolling Stone* put him on a front cover with Bob Marley and Dickie Jobson later made an eponymous film about him. He died in 2016.

CULTURE: Classic roots harmony trio who found international success with their stunning *Two Sevens Clash* album.

DILLINGER: One of a host of Jamaican 'toasters' who preceded rap music by a good decade. Most famous for his song 'Cocaine In My Brain' from *CB 200*.

TYRONE DOWNIE: A child keyboard prodigy, he was already a sought-after session player before becoming the youngest member of The Wailers. Tyrone died in 2022.

SLY DUNBAR & ROBBIE SHAKESPEARE: Jamaica's most famous rhythm section. Setting up their own label, Taxi, they proved highly innovative – particularly in their use of new technology – and pioneered the dancehall sound that would dominate Jamaican music in the Eighties and Nineties. They worked with everyone from Junior Delgado and Peter Tosh to Bob Dylan. Robbie died in 2021.

NEVILLE GARRICK: See *Contributors*, page 6.

ANTONIO 'GILLIE' GILBERT: See *Contributors*, page 6.

MARCIA GRIFFITHS: Sometimes called Jamaica's first lady of song, she was already famous for her hits as one half of Bob and Marcia when she teamed up with Rita Marley and Judy Mowatt to form The I-Three.

TOOTS HIBBERT: A star in Jamaica from the early Sixties when his group The Maytals cut hits for all the leading producers including Sir Coxsone Dodd, Randy's, Beverley's and Prince Buster. Toots died in 2020.

GREGORY ISAACS: One of Jamaica's most consistently popular singers, his mid-Seventies records like 'Rasta Business' were firm cultural statements, but he was to sustain his success over the coming decades primarily with 'lovers' tunes. Gregory died in 2010.

RITA MARLEY: Bob's wife and respected solo artist in her own right. One third of vocal trio The I-Three she recorded and toured with Bob from the *Natty Dread* album onwards.

JUNIOR MARVIN: See *Contributors*, page 6.

RAS MICHAEL: One of few to take Nyahbingi music to commercial success. Nyahbingi is the music traditionally played at Rastafarian grounations and is characterised by chants and hand drumming.

JACOB MILLER & INNER CIRCLE: In the Seventies Jacob Miller was second in popularity only to Bob Marley. Albums like *Wanted* and *Jacob 'Killer' Miller* had people touting him as Bob's natural successor. He died in a car crash in 1980.

JUDY MOWATT: Also a respected solo artist, joined with Rita Marley and Marcia Griffiths to form The I-Three.

AUGUSTUS PABLO: Fantastically talented musician and producer whose inimitable style has influenced so many. Perhaps most famous for his melodica playing and the groundbreaking dub of *King Tubby Meets Rockers Uptown*. He died in 1999.

ALVIN 'SEECO' PATTERSON: First met Bob, Peter and Bunny in the Kingston ghettos. An elder Rasta and expert hand drummer, he was responsible for taking the fledgling Wailers to their audition with Sir Coxsone Dodd and later joined the band as percussionist. He died in 2021.

LEE 'SCRATCH' PERRY: See *Contributors*, page 6.

PETER TOSH: Boyhood friend of Bob's and founder member of The Wailers. Later had a successful solo career with albums like *Legalize It*, signed to the Rolling Stones' record label and recorded 'Don't Look Back' with Mick Jagger. He was killed in 1987.

TRINITY: Another toaster of enormous popularity in the Seventies. The title song of his *Three Piece Suit* album anticipated the Eighties' dancehall style. He died in 2021.

KING TUBBY: Pioneering producer and engineer said to have invented the 'dub' style. Most producers and artists sent their work to Tubby at some point for remixing, an art he refined decades before it would become the norm using self-adapted machinery that would seem primitive by today's standards. He died in 1989.

U-ROY: Sometimes referred to as the 'Originator', he wasn't the first DJ to toast over records, but his popularity was unprecedented. Inspired every DJ that followed in his substantial wake.

BUNNY WAILER: The third member of the original Wailers vocal trio. His solo album *Blackheart Man* is considered an all-time classic by reggae aficionados. He died in 2021.

KATE SIMON WOULD LIKE TO THANK:

Bob Marley and The Wailers, and all the legends of reggae showcased herein.
Brian Roylance for giving me the opportunity to publish these images so beautifully.
Robby Elson who had a feel for the subject matter as much as I did, and put his whole self into the editing and interviewing he did for this book.
We worked as a team.
To Chris Murray, loyal friend, and head of Govinda Gallery. Chris shared the vision of this book from the beginning and kept it on track.
He saw how good it could be even before I did.
Debbie Keith for making the most exquisite black and white prints.
Meegan Voss: shortly after receiving the rough draft, Meegan came into the project like a gift from Heaven – her support, intelligence and editorial skills enabled me to finish the book.
Patti Smith for writing such a beautiful Introduction.
Fred Schruers for his beautiful new piece 'Hail', and his article from *Tuff Gong* originally published in *The Washington Post*, and for interviewing Chris Blackwell so brilliantly. Fred, you are irie.
Dave Brolan and Dagon James for their friendship and support.
Tom Danziger for his intelligence and legal guidance.
Thomas Manzi for all his help.
Hudson Bohr for her studio help.
Chris Blackwell for sending me on the Exodus Tour.
Steve Jordan: this entire effort was immeasurably enriched by his musical insight, his willingness to corral a gallery of esteemed fellow musicians, and his unfailing, fervent enthusiasm.
Elizabeth Barraclough for interviewing Aston 'Family Man' Barrett for this book and for her input and advice innumerable times during its creation.
Roger Steffens for interviewing me and being a walking encyclopedia of information which he is always generous in sharing.
Randall Grass, Head of Shanachie Entertainment. Randall's intellect, taste and familiarity with the subject matter are unparalleled.
Thank you for your input, and your insightful interview.
Glenn O'Brien, a frequent collaborator, for his literary contribution to this book, and for many years of friendship.
Michael Zilkha, one of the most generous and informed collectors I have ever come across and a total delight as a person.
Patti Palladin for her loyalty and friendship.
Jim DeRogatis for the piece he contributed to this book and his exquisite writing for the *Chicago Sun Times*.
Steven Van Zandt for his deeply felt observations.
Bruce Springsteen for his eloquent words.
Paul Simonon for his friendship and reggae expertise; Jennifer Kessler; Nick Roylance for his beautiful film of me, and his kind nature; Catherine Roylance for her early enthusiasm for this project; Don Letts; Dickie Jobson; John Morthland for giving us permission to use Lester Bangs's words; Neville Garrick for his inspired art direction and the interview he gave for this book; and Antonio 'Gillie' Gilbert, for his contributions to the book.

To Andi Ostrowe, my friend and Patti Smith aide de camp, for her help and encouragement. Anna Capaldi, Ann Hogan, Louie Chaban, Judy Nylon, Richard Boch, Maia Norman, Michelle Martin, Alice Wilson, Simon Browne, Zoe Stewart, and Sidney Allison for their continued friendship and support.
Finally, my brother Paul Simon and my sister-in-law Jennifer Brown; my niece Emily Simon.

In Memoriam:
Dr. Samuel Simon M.D., my father
Bob Marley
Albert Grossman
Carl Apfelschnitt
William S. Burroughs
Joe Strummer
Glenn O'Brien
Lois Marino
Debbie Geller

GENESIS PUBLICATIONS WOULD LIKE TO THANK:

Along with all those mentioned above, Genesis would like to thank all of the contributors, without whom this book would have been impossible.
Special thanks go to Fred Schruers – for his essays and for interviewing Chris Blackwell, and to Roger Steffens for allowing the publishers to visit his astonishing reggae archives; for his endless enthusiasm for, not to mention knowledge of, Bob Marley and reggae; and for freely sharing all and more for the purposes of this book. Many years of research went into compiling the complete chronology of Bob Marley and The Wailers' recordings, and we are grateful to Roger that he has allowed us to publish it here.
His interviews – published in *Beat* magazine – as well as his website, lectures and email correspondence, have informed the research of this book at every stage.
Thanks to Patti Smith and Andi Ostrowe; Bruce Springsteen; Chris Murray, Virginia Lohle and Bob Gruen; Bruno Blum and Elizabeth Barraclough for invaluable material from Joe Strummer and Family Man respectively; Lucinda Strummer; Patti Palladin; Ryan Speers; Simon Padmore; Dylan Taite – you are missed; Lenny Kravitz and Keith Richards for their wonderful contributions to this new edition; Craig Fruin and the team at CSM Management; Jane Rose; and Thomas Manzi.
Thanks also to our editors Robby Elson and Alexandra Rigby-Wild, Nicky Page for the wonderful design, and the Genesis team.
Finally, thanks to Kate Simon for dedicating so much of herself to the cause; working with such a wonderful archive of photos is not work at all. Thanks for opening your door to us – and for having the best tea in New York!
One Love.